The Tavern

A Play in Two Acts

by George M. Cohan

Suggested by a play entitled
The Choice of a Super-Man
by Cora Dick Gantt

A SAMUEL FRENCH ACTING EDITION

FOUNDED 1830

New York Hollywood London Toronto

SAMUELFRENCH.COM

Copyright © 1920, 1933 by George M. Cohan
Copyright © 1947, 1961 by Agnes M. Cohan

ALL RIGHTS RESERVED

CAUTION: Professionals and amateurs are hereby warned that *THE TAVERN* is subject to a Licensing Fee. It is fully protected under the copyright laws of the United States of America, the British Commonwealth, including Canada, and all other countries of the Copyright Union. All rights, including professional, amateur, motion picture, recitation, lecturing, public reading, radio broadcasting, television and the rights of translation into foreign languages are strictly reserved. In its present form the play is dedicated to the reading public only.

The amateur live stage performance rights to *THE TAVERN* are controlled exclusively by Samuel French, Inc., and licensing arrangements and performance licenses must be secured well in advance of presentation. PLEASE NOTE that amateur Licensing Fees are set upon application in accordance with your producing circumstances. When applying for a licensing quotation and a performance license please give us the number of performances intended, dates of production, your seating capacity and admission fee. Licensing Fees are payable one week before the opening performance of the play to Samuel French, Inc., at 45 W. 25th Street, New York, NY 10010.

Licensing Fee of the required amount must be paid whether the play is presented for charity or gain and whether or not admission is charged.

Stock licensing fees quoted upon application to Samuel French, Inc.

For all other rights than those stipulated above, apply to: Samuel French, Inc.

Particular emphasis is laid on the question of amateur or professional readings, permission and terms for which must be secured in writing from Samuel French, Inc.

Copying from this book in whole or in part is strictly forbidden by law, and the right of performance is not transferable.

Whenever the play is produced the following notice must appear on all programs, printing and advertising for the play: "Produced by special arrangement with Samuel French, Inc."

Due authorship credit must be given on all programs, printing and advertising for the play.

No one shall commit or authorize any act or omission by which the copyright of, or the right to copyright, this play may be impaired.
No one shall make any changes in this play for the purpose of production.
Publication of this play does not imply availability for performance. Both amateurs and professionals considering a production are strongly advised in their own interests to apply to Samuel French, Inc., for written permission before starting rehearsals, advertising, or booking a theatre.
No part of this book may be reproduced, stored in a retrieval system, or transmitted in any form, by any means, now known or yet to be invented, including mechanical, electronic, photocopying, recording, videotaping, or otherwise, without the prior written permission of the publisher.

ISBN 978-0-573-61635-8   Printed in U.S.A.   #22023

Program of "The Tavern," as presented at the Fulton Theatre, New York:

CAST OF CHARACTERS
(In the order of their appearance)

THE TAVERN KEEPER'S SON	*Theodore Newton*
THE HIRED GIRL	*Kathleen Niday*
THE TAVERN KEEPER	*Robert Middlemass*
THE HIRED MAN	*Joseph Allen*
THE VAGABOND	*George M. Cohan*
THE WOMAN	*Mary Philips*
THE GOVERNOR	*Jack Leslie*
THE GOVERNOR'S WIFE	*Lida MacMillan*
THE GOVERNOR'S DAUGHTER	*Isabel Baring*
THE FIANCE	*Douglas MacPherson*
THE SHERIFF	*Edward F. Nannery*
THE SHERIFF'S MEN	*Jack Williams* / *Dan Carey* / *Manuel Duarte*
THE ATTENDANT	*Harold Healy*

The play is in two acts.

(Intermission 12 minutes.)

The action of the play takes place in ZACCHEUS FREEMAN'S *Tavern.*

CHARACTERS
(In the order of their first appearance)

ZACH, *the Tavern Keeper's son.*
SALLY, *the hired girl.*
FREEMAN, *the Tavern Keeper.*
WILLUM, *the hired man.*
THE VAGABOND.
VIOLET, *the woman.*
LAMSON, *the Governor.*
MRS. LAMSON, *the Governor's wife.*
VIRGINIA, *the Governor's daughter.*
TOM ALLEN, *the fiance.*
THE SHERIFF.
EZRA, *the Sheriff's man.*
JOSHUA, *the Sheriff's other man.*
TONY, *the Sheriff's third man.*
STEVENS, *the attendant.*

The play is in two acts

The action takes place in Freeman's Tavern.

COSTUMES

The Vagabond: *High tan boots, corduroy pants, white shirt open at the throat; dark vest; long heavy patched coat; large dark brown hat; long dark green cape; staff.*

The Governor: *Patent leather shoes; tan trousers strapped under the shoes; double breasted vest; velvet coat (Southern period); soft black hat; long black cape; white shirt and black stock tie.*

The Fiance: *Grey trousers and coat (Southern period); patent leather shoes; soft black hat; white ruffled sleeves and shirt front; black stock; long cape.*

The Hired Man: *Old tan boots; short brown trousers; old green coat; colored shirt; brown vest; soft brown hat.*

Tavern Keeper: *Slippers; grey woolen stockings; short white apron; white ballet shirt; long, brown square-cut great coat; large black soft hat; blue knickerbockers; black vest; boots (to wear when he goes out).*

Zach: *Rough boots; short ballet shirt; short red coat; heavy brown coat; soft hat; grey pants.*

The Sheriff: *Black pants; white ballet shirt; dark pea jacket; rough coat; large black hat; high boots; sheriff's badge.*

Hired Girl: *Brown dress, white lace collar; blue apron; black stockings and slippers.*

COSTUMES

GOVERNOR'S WIFE: *Dress and cape; lace veil to throw over head. Changes to evening dress; not modern.*

THE WOMAN: *Plain grey dress and dark cape.*

ATTENDANT: *Black pants, black coat, long black cape; soft brown hat; high black boots.*

SHERIFF'S MEN: *Tan and brown pants; white shirts; short jackets; black capes; brown hats; rough boots.*

GOVERNOR'S DAUGHTER: *Italian peasant style dress; black stockings and slippers.*

THE TAVERN

ACT ONE

Scene: *The interior of* Zaccheus Freeman's *Tavern. Clock is set at* 12.

THUNDER started about 10 seconds before Curtain rises. At rise CRASH is heard. (CRASH consists of Pistol SHOT, THUNDER and WIND machines and LIGHTNING.)

As the Curtain rises the stage is bare. A furious STORM is raging outside. Whenever the door is opened during the action of the play, a CRASH is heard. The door upstage c. *is unbarred at rise.*

After about 8 seconds the door up c. *flies open and* Zach, *the Innkeeper's son, enters, his arms filled with logs of wood. (CRASH.)*

He slams the door shut, bars it and stands leaning against it trembling with fright. He places the logs in a wood-box near the fireplace and stands looking at window up L. *at back.*

(LIGHTNING.)

After a few seconds, he goes up to the window and peers out, listening for some sound. He then takes off his hat and coat and hangs them on a peg R. *of door* C. *He again goes to the window (LIGHTNING) and looks fearfully out into the night; then turns front, thinking. After a second's thought he crosses to the stairs and calls softly:*

ZACH. *(At foot of stairs)* Hist! Hist! *(Looking nervously toward window, he again calls)* Sally! Sally!

SALLY. *(Entering at head of stairs R.)* Is that you, Zach?

ZACH. *(Quieting her; his back to the audience, still looking in fright toward the window up L.)* Hush!

SALLY. *(She comes down R.C., staring at ZACH as he tries to "hush" her)* What frightened you, Zach?

ZACH. I'm not frightened. I never get frightened.

SALLY. You're as white as a sheet.

ZACH. *(Trembling)* Am I? Then it's the storm.

SALLY. You're trembling. What's the matter?

ZACH. It's the cold. *(Crossing to L.C.)* It's bitter outside.

SALLY. Don't lie, Zach; something frightened you; what is it?

ZACH. Hush! *(Motions her to be quiet; goes to door C. and listens, then returns to her)* There's someone out there—hiding—crouching down and hiding. (SALLY *moves closer to him, frightened now.*) I went to the woodshed for logs. I heard something moving. I could almost swear I heard the breathing.

SALLY. *(Grabbing* ZACH *in her fright)* It might have been the wind.

ZACH. So I thought at first, but I struck a match and saw a creeping shadow on the wall as plainly as I see you now. *(He looks over his shoulder nervously.)*

SALLY. *(Pause; she moves closer to* ZACH*)* Someone seeking shelter from the storm.

ZACH. Then why in the woodshed? Why not here in the tavern?

SALLY. *(Pause; looks toward window)* Who could it be?

ZACH. *(Up to L. side of the window)* No friend, that's sure; someone with an evil mind and bad thoughts. I feel it, Sally.

SALLY. Zach!

ZACH. They do say that nights such as this bring courage to the blackest hearts.

SALLY. *(Moving slightly R.)* I'll call your father.

ZACH. *(Crosses and stops her)* No, no; he'll say I'm frightened.

SALLY. *(After a slight pause)* You are.

ZACH. Think so? *(Gathers his courage, goes to L.U. corner and gets a shotgun and comes back to SALLY.)*

SALLY. *(Screams)* Zach! *(He turns to her)* What are you going to do?

ZACH. If it's a murder they're going to play at I'll take a hand in the game myself. *(CRASH. SALLY screams and falls on her knees up C. They hold the picture a moment.)*

FREEMAN. *(Pause; off, upstairs)* What was that? *(He enters on stairs and stands on landing, looking down at ZACH and SALLY. Finally he notices the shotgun ZACH is still holding)* Did you fire a shot, Zach?

ZACH. No, Father, 'twas a clap of thunder.

FREEMAN. *(Coming downstairs to C.)* Egad, I thought the world had come to an end. *(Goes to SALLY, who is still on her knees, mumbling.)* Sally, what is this? *(Turns to ZACH)* And you, Zach, with a shotgun. Come, an explanation at once.

ZACH. She's frightened, Father.

FREEMAN. Frightened? At what, the storm? There have been worse nights than this.

SALLY. *(Gets to her feet)* No, no, no; it's not

the storm, Master, it's the creeping shadow on the wall.

FREEMAN. A creeping shadow? *(Pause)* What is this tomfoolery?

SALLY. Tell him, Zach.

FREEMAN. Come, boy, what is this? Has the girl gone mad?

ZACH. No, it's the truth, Father. There *was* a creeping shadow on the wall of the woodshed. I just came from there with the logs.

FREEMAN. What did you see?

ZACH. A figured crouched behind the woodpile.

FREEMAN. A figure crouched behind the—— Are you sure?

ZACH. I'd swear it.

FREEMAN. *(Looks toward the window; then turns to* ZACH*)* Did he answer when you called?

ZACH. I didn't call. *(Lowers his head)* I thought it best to wait and——

FREEMAN. Simpleton! You were afraid.

ZACH. Afraid? No!

SALLY. *(To* FREEMAN*)* He was—he trembled like a leaf, Master.

ZACH. It's not the truth.

FREEMAN. Enough of this! Come, the weapon. (ZACH *hands him the gun and steps back.)* I'll soon rid the shed of shadows. *(Takes a step upstage* C. *THUNDER.)*

ZACH. The storm is raging, Father.

FREEMAN. *(Stops; turns to* SALLY*)* My greatcoat, Sally, quick! *(He puts the shotgun on table* L.C.; *gets his boots* R. *of table near window up* L.*)*

SALLY. Yes good Master. *(She rushes upstairs and off* R. FREEMAN *sits at table* L.C.; *takes off his slippers and puts on his boots.)*

ZACH. *(Pause; stands at father's* R.*)* Give me the gun, Father; let me do the thing if it must be done. It may mean a fight to the death.

FREEMAN. Then better my old life than your youth.

ZACH. But I have the strength for a struggle.

FREEMAN. There is no struggle when both are armed; it's think fast and shoot straight. *(He rises and puts his slippers R. of table up L.)*

ZACH. *(Coming to front of table L.C.)* Father, I implore you not to go.

FREEMAN. Don't waste words.

ZACH. Then I go, too.

FREEMAN. I forbid it. *(Takes his hat from peg R.C.; puts in on and calls up the stairs to SALLY)* Be quick, Sally, my coat. *(Comes down C.)*

SALLY. *(Rushing on with FREEMAN'S coat)* I'm coming, good Master.

FREEMAN. *(Donning coat)* Dead or alive, I'll take him, whoever he is. *(Pause)* Should he prove to be of the band that held up the coach a fortnight ago, the fat reward will help to pay the debts that weigh me down. 'Twill be a good night's work, my lad, if that comes true. *(He crosses; picks up gun from table L.C. and moves upstage a step.)*

ZACH. Take me along, Father, please.

FREEMAN. I've said no. *(Quite a lot of THUNDER.)* My mind is set. *(He goes upstage C.)*

ZACH. *(Up with FREEMAN)* The storm is blinding.

FREEMAN. I'll grope my way. *(CRASH. He stands C., motioning to ZACH to unbar door. ZACH unbars the door and throws it open. FREEMAN lowers his head and fights his way out against the wind and rain. ZACH slams the door shut, but does not bar it.)*

SALLY. You shouldn't have let him go, Zach.

ZACH. *(Crosses and peers out of the window)* He'd have it that way. His word is law.

SALLY. Do you think the shadow is armed?

ZACH. *(Crossing to SALLY)* Of course. Would

an honest man be prowling about on a night like this?

SALLY. Your father might be killed.

ZACH. *(Crossing to* SALLY*)* Killed! Sally, I'd die of grief. *(Starts up* C.*)*

SALLY. Then what would become of me? I couldn't live without you, Zach. *(Clings to him, sobbing)* I love you so, Zach. You know I do.

ZACH. *(Pushing her from him)* Don't do that; this is no time for lally-gagging. *(Pause)* There's danger near. *(Goes* R.*, facing front)* I feel there is *(One pistol SHOT.* SALLY *is sobbing.* SALLY *screams; hugs* ZACH *for protection. They cling to each other,* SALLY *sobbing hysterically.)* Hush! Be quiet!

SALLY. *(Sobbing)* I'm afraid, Zach; I'm afraid!

ZACH. Hush! One shot—he must have got his man. *(Pause; another SHOT offstage.* SALLY *screams.)* That's the reply. It's a duel, Sally.

SALLY. *(Hugging close to* ZACH*)* Zach!

WILLUM. *(Runs on from stairs and comes to landing)* What's the shootin' for? *(*ZACH *goes to window up* L. SALLY *to* R.*)* Who's a-shootin' that way?

ZACH. Be quiet, Willum.

WILLUM. *(Comes down to* SALLY*, raising his voice)* What's the shootin' for? *(*ZACH *comes down below table* L.C.*)*

SALLY. Go to bed, Willum. Go to bed, there's danger near.

WILLUM. *(Over to* ZACH*)* What's all the shootin' for?

ZACH. Be quiet, Willum.

WILLUM. *(Back to* SALLY*)* What's all the shootin' for?

SALLY. Be quiet, Willum.

WILLUM. *(Goes to the stairs; mounts two or three; returns; then back to a position between*

ZACH *and* SALLY) Ah, you two together ag'in, eh? Caught you at it ag'in, eh? Didn't I? Crept down to spoon, I suppose, when you thought we were all asleep. *(Crossing to* SALLY*)* The Master told you to keep away from his boy, didn't he? *(Goes back to* ZACH*)* Your father warned you not to spark with that gal. I heard him when he said it. I'm a-goin' to tell him, do you understand? I'm a-goin' to tell him, that I caught you here alone in the dead of night. *(Goes to the foot of stairs and yells)* Master—Master—Master Freeman.

ZACH. *(Rushes to* WILLUM: *grabs him by the throat, and brings him to his knees)* Damn you, Willum, I'll choke you till you hush. *(Tightens his grip on* WILLUM'S *throat.)*

SALLY. *(Goes to* ZACH'S R., *pleadingly)* Don't, Zach, don't, you'll kill him.

WILLUM. *(After* ZACH *has released him, and thrown him to the ground)* Tryin' to take her away from me, wasn't you?

ZACH. Hold your tongue, Willum. *(Crosses* L., *away from* WILLUM.*)*

WILLUM. *(Arising to his feet)* You know she's all I care about. She knows it, too, I've told her a thousand times.

SALLY. You're a crazy man, Willum.

WILLUM. I'm a-goin' to tell the Master. He'll put an end to your sparkin', see if he don't. *(He goes up to the stairs.* SALLY *down back of armchair.)* Master! Master! Master Freeman! *(*ZACH *goes up* L.*)*

FREEMAN. *(Enters* C., *blinded by the storm.* CRASH. *He leans against the door; shakes the raindrops from his hat; places it on table up* L.*; closes and bars the door)* Who calls me? *(He comes down* C. WILLUM *crosses to* FREEMAN *on his entrance and now follows him down.* ZACH *moves to* L. *of table.)*

WILLUM. *(Down with* FREEMAN*)* It's I, Willum. I caught 'em again, Master, they were here alone.

FREEMAN. *(Looking sternly at* ZACH*)* What?

WILLUM. You remember you warned them. They didn't obey. They were here alone.

ZACH. Be quiet, Willum.

WILLUM. *(Blubbering)* He tried to choke me when I swore I'd tell.

FREEMAN. To your room, Willum. *(Goes to fireplace, putting gun in lower corner.)*

WILLUM. *(Going to* FREEMAN*)* You warned them, but they didn't obey.

FREEMAN. *(Taking off his outer coat)* To your room, I said. *(Stands, warming his hands.)*

WILLUM. *(Starts upstairs; comes down above armchair* R.*)* I caught them. They were in each other's arms—like the lovers you read about. *(He goes up to foot of stairs.* FREEMAN *looks at him.)* Nice carryings on for a respectable tavern. Watch out, good Master, they'll bring dishonor on your name. *(He looks meaningly at* SALLY.*)*

SALLY. *(To* WILLUM*)* To your room, the Master said. *(She gets* FREEMAN'S *coat and hangs it on the peg* R. *of door* C.*.)*

WILLUM. *(Back to* FREEMAN*)* I heard the shots. What was the shootin' for?

FREEMAN. In the morning you'll know. Goodnight, Willum.

WILLUM. Goodnight, sir. *(He goes upstairs; turns and addresses* ZACH*)* You keep away from that gal, that's all I ask. I love that gal.

FREEMAN. To your room, Willum.

WILLUM. But I love that gal. *(Sticks his tongue out at* SALLY *and "bahs." Exits at upstairs to* R.*)*

ZACH. *(Goes down in front of table* L.C.*)* What happened, Father? Did you see the man?

FREEMAN. Yes, he returned fire and fled into the

night. Some harmless fool, no doubt, who ran to cover from the storm.

SALLY. *(Coming down* R.C.*)* Then he's gone?

FREEMAN. Yes, he's gone. *(Turns on* SALLY*)* Now *you* go; I want a word with my son.

SALLY. Yes, Master. *(Goes to foot of stairs.* ZACH *turns, facing her.)*

FREEMAN. In the morning I'll have my say to you, my lass.

SALLY. *(Coming down* R.*)* What Willum said was not true, Master. He only imagined that Zach and I were——

FREEMAN. *(Interrupts)* To your room. We'll discuss this in the morning. *(*FREEMAN *turns to fire and warms his hands. Back to the fire.)*

SALLY. *(As she goes upstairs)* Yes. Good Master.

FREEMAN. *(Has crossed up* R. *to door; then down* C.*)* Shall I go on forever forbidding this affair, or must I turn the girl out for good and all?

ZACH. *(Crossing* C. *to* FREEMAN*)* We weren't sparking, Father, so help me.

FREEMAN. Then, how came the girl downstairs?

ZACH. I called to her to come.

FREEMAN. And why?

ZACH. I'd just seen the crouching figure in the shed and——

FREEMAN. —and trembled like a leaf. What Sally said, then, was true. My son *is* a coward.

ZACH. No. No. Father.

FREEMAN. Then, why did you call to her?

ZACH. To warn her of danger.

FREEMAN. Ah, she was first in your mind.

ZACH. No, Father, she wasn't.

FREEMAN. Don't lie, son. I can read your very thoughts. *(*ZACH *lowers head.)* You're at the petticoat age—slavey or queen—no choice in your desire, I know. *(Crosses* R. *to fireplace.)*

ZACH. You're wrong, Father.

FREEMAN. Perhaps. But for fear I'm right, we'll bundle her off, bag and baggage, in the morning. *(Turns from ZACH.)*

ZACH. *(Taking look at the stairs)* That would be cruel, she's a homeless child.

FREEMAN. *(Turns to ZACH)* Aha! There's pity in your heart.

ZACH. Only pity.

FREEMAN. First symptoms. Next will come infatuation. Beware, son. Don't buckle on to a beggar to give a squalling kid a name.

ZACH. Father, don't say such things.

FREEMAN. *(Places his hand affectionately on ZACH's shoulder)* 'Tis for your own good that I speak. There are wealthy wives to be had. Get lands and cattle in trade for your name. It can be done, my son.

ZACH. *(Very earnestly. Looking forward)* Perhaps—but when I marry, 'twill be for love.

FREEMAN. Ah. You've said enough. I know now that the wench has wheedled you into the very thought. Out of the tavern she goes at dawn. *(Crosses R. to fireplace.)*

ZACH. Then I go with her.

FREEMAN. *(Turns to ZACH)* Oh, so my guess was right, you love the brat.

ZACH. She's not a brat.

FREEMAN. Take care what you say to me.

ZACH. Take care what you say to her.

FREEMAN. I'm your father.

ZACH. Don't make me forget that fact.

FREEMAN. *(Threateningly)* Weakling—ingrate.

ZACH. Call me what you like, but I'm damned if I'll have her slurred on my account.

FREEMAN. You dare defy me?

ZACH. Yes.

FREEMAN. To your room. *(They stand staring at*

each other defiantly throughout the CRASH and THUNDER. As it subsides, FREEMAN *speaks)* I told you to go to your room.

ZACH. *(Slowly making his way toward stairs)* I'm a-goin'. *(After reaching foot of stairs)* I'm a-goin'.

(VAGABOND *KNOCKS on* C. *door.* ZACH *and* FREEMAN *look wonderingly at each other.* VAGABOND *after a pause repeats the KNOCK.* FREEMAN *has gone to fireplace to get shotgun and holds it in readiness, facing the door. There is a roll of THUNDER preceding first knock, until* FREEMAN *speaks. Then it is resumed.)*

FREEMAN. See who it is? (ZACH *moves upstage; unbars and opens* C. *door. CRASH.)*
VAGABOND. *(Enters and comes downstage* C. ZACH *moves over* L. *to* R. *of* L.C. *table.)* Greetings, my friends. 'Tis a glorious storm, is it not? By God, gentlemen, it was worth being born to have lived on a night like this.
FREEMAN. Throw up your hands.
VAGABOND. What?
FREEMAN. Throw up your hands.
VAGABOND. What a childish idea.
FREEMAN. Throw up your hands, or I'll shoot.
VAGABOND. Shoot and be hanged. If you shoot, you'll kill, if you kill, you'll hang. That's the penalty, I believe, and so, my dear sir, if you have the insane desire to rid yourself of the responsibilities of this life, by a spectacular climb to the gallows, why not shoot someone worth while? It's who you murder that counts. That is—if you'd have the world celebrate the date of your execution. *(He turns up and leisurely surveys the room.* ZACH *drops down* L. *of table.)*
FREEMAN. *(After a pause)* Who are you?

VAGABOND. *(Turns to* FREEMAN *with a laugh)* Ha, ha, that's just it! Who *am* I? Who *was* he and why did the madman kill him? Those questions would be on everbody's lips. It would be a waste of time and ammunition. *(He takes gun from his pocket and throws it in the armchair* R. FREEMAN *raises his gun.)* Don't be alarmed, it's the only weapon I ever carried—the only one. You may search me if you think I'm cheating.

FREEMAN. *(After a pause)* What is it you want?

VAGABOND. A smile and a kind word, that is all I ask of any man.

FREEMAN. What sort of a man *are* you?

VAGABOND. A fugitive.

FREEMAN. A fugitive—from the law?

VAGABOND. No—from my own thoughts.

FREEMAN. *Where* are you bound for?

VAGABOND. I've arrived.

FREEMAN. Where do you think you are?

VAGABOND. Ah, 'tis well I know where I am. I'm at the beginning—and end of the earth.

FREEMAN. The beginning and end of the *earth!*

VAGABOND. The beginning and end of the earth. Wherever I am it's just that, for I never return to any spot until I've circled the globe, and so you see, my starting point is really my destination. *(Indicates with circling motion of stick)* Do you follow me?

FREEMAN. Are you crazy?

VAGABOND. Yes—as crazy as you think I **am**—and as sane as you think you are.

FREEMAN. I don't understand you at all.

VAGABOND. I never met the man who did. *(Going to* C.*)* But don't be alarmed, I'm harmless, quite harmless—I'm as harmless as the little orphan girl that you threatened to turn from your door at dawn. (ZACH *moves to* R. *of table* L.C.*)*

FREEMAN. What do you mean?

VAGABOND. That I've had my ear glued to the crack of that door for the last few minutes listening with delight to the manly protests of your son against the suggestion that he trade his name for lands and cattle. *(He turns to* ZACH*)* I congratulate you, my boy. No man could put into words a more noble expression than the romantic, heroic, time-worn, old-fashioned utterance: "When I marry 'twill be for love." I burst out laughing when you said it. 'Twas then I made up my mind to have a look at you both. *(Turns to* FREEMAN*)* And so I knocked and when you—*(Indicating* ZACH*)*—lifted the bar, I knew well enough I was walking into the muzzle of a shotgun, but I had no fear—no fear, for I knew our friend was no expert aim, having already witnessed a rather poor exhibition of marksmanship in the woodshed.

ZACH. *(After a pause)* Then it was *you* hiding in the shed?

VAGABOND. *(Turns to* ZACH*)* 'Twas I—slumbering peacefully in the loft when you stumbled over a load of logs and ran away. *(Laughs)* How I laughed at your clumsiness. *(Laughs)* And then the thought that you'd scraped your shins amused me the more and I laughed again. *(Laughs)* And then your father came—your father came with his famous shotgun. And oh, Lord, how I laughed at him! *(Laughs. Moves* R.C., *to* FREEMAN*)* What a damn poor judge of distance you are, my friend. *(Laughs.)*

FREEMAN. *(After a pause)* But I shot in the air. Can you say as much when you missed me on the return fire?

VAGABOND. Ah, you judge me wrongly. I did not return the fire. *(Pointing to the gun in the armchair)* That weapon is not mine. No. 'Twas the shot that missed you as you dashed through the door out into the open that made me realize for the first time that I was not the *only occupant* of the woodshed.

ZACH. *(Slight pause)* Another man in the shed?

VAGABOND. No—a woman.

FREEMAN. *A woman!*

VAGABOND. What I say is true, my friend. 'Twas a woman shot at you. She missed. She missed and was aiming for another try at your fleeing figure when I leaped from the loft and wrested the weapon from her grasp. *(Raises clenched hand aloft and shakes it)* So you see, if life means anything at all to you, you owe me a debt—owe me a debt of gratitude that can only be repaid with a drink of brandy.

FREEMAN. So, this is your way of begging a drink.

VAGABOND. Come, surely, I've earned a gill of the stuff—if all I've said be true.

FREEMAN. So, 'tis the craving for drink that's driven you mad.

VAGABOND. No, no, my craving for drink is satisfied at any running stream or babbling brook. *(Indicates with stick)* I need neither stimulant for mind nor body. 'Tis for a woman I appeal. *(Turns to ZACH)* Come, boy, the brandy. If your father fails me I'll look to you to be the same gallant young man you were in your stand for the little slavey.

ZACH. Is the woman ill?

VAGABOND. Tired, weary, exhausted, driven from the roads by the downpour of rain and the sting of the hail; drenched to the skin and trembling with fear and cold.

ZACH. Father, this may be so.

FREEMAN. What of that—'tis not a charity shop.

VAGABOND. Would you see the woman die?

FREEMAN. It's a trick; there *is* no woman.

VAGABOND. No woman? You doubt my word?

Very well. *(Starts upstage C.)* Come, see for yourself.

FREEMAN. *(Levelling the gun at the* VAGABOND*)* Stop! *(The* VAGABOND *stops and turns to* FREEMAN*)* You'll not leave this tavern until I say the word.

VAGABOND. Oh, am I to be a lodger? Ah, 'tis well. *(Comes downstage)* But do see for yourself that there is a woman, an almost prostrate woman in the shed.

FREEMAN. *(Picks up the* VAGABOND'S *gun from the armchair; crosses and hands it to* ZACH*)* I'll go alone. *(He goes upstage, followed by* ZACH.*)*

VAGABOND. *(Going up R.)* So be it.

FREEMAN. *(Puts his shotgun R. of C. door; gets his overcoat on peg R. of the door and puts it on)* Keep him covered, son, there may be a reward for this—braggart.

VAGABOND. *(Laughs lightly)* Suspicious even of me. Do I look like a bandit?

FREEMAN. You do—and I think you *are* one.

VAGABOND. A compliment, my friend. To be thought of as anything but a vagabond is indeed a most decided compliment. *(He makes* FREEMAN *a sweeping bow.)*

FREEMAN. Keep him covered, son, till I return.

VAGABOND. *(Mockingly)* Keep him covered, son, till I return.

ZACH. Trust me, Father. *(*FREEMAN *unbars the door and goes out into the storm.* ZACH *closes and bars the door; turns and covers the* VAGABOND *with the revolver. CRASH.)*

VAGABOND. *(Puts his hat and cloak on table up R.; moves down to the fireplace; turns and sees* ZACH *pointing the gun at him. Does a step; weaves body; makes mock rush as though to attack* ZACH *and laughs.)* Lower your gun, lower your gun, my boy. Don't strain your nerves.

ZACH. *(With determination)* I must obey my father. *(He comes down* C. *a step.)*

VAGABOND. Yes. And yet you defied him but a moment ago. Come, Zach, now, you're a better judge of character than he. A fair question; beneath this somewhat shabby exterior—*(Indicates attire)*—can you not trace something unmistakably refined and genteel?

ZACH. I could almost swear you were a gentleman.

VAGABOND. *(Curtsies)* I thank you.

ZACH. Yet you act and look like a vagabond.

VAGABOND. *(Curtsies)* Again I thank you. *(He moves over to the fire.)*

ZACH. Which are you?

VAGABOND. *(Going* R.C., *looking about the room)* Neither—both. *(Shouts word "both."* ZACH *backs away as the* VAGABOND *comes to* C.*)* But what does it matter so long as I promise you that I'll not attempt to escape? As a matter of fact, I rather like this old tavern. It has atmosphere, great dramatic possibilities, and besides—*(Going to* R.C.*)*—it's far more comfortable than the loft of the shed. *(He drops into chair* R.*)*

ZACH. *(After a pause he goes to the* VAGABOND*)* Is the woman really there?

VAGABOND. She *was*—I imagine she is. I hardly think she'd venture out in such a wonderful storm.

ZACH. Where is she from?

VAGABOND. Heaven, perhaps—(SALLY *enters on stairs and looks over bannisters at* VAGABOND.*)* —on her way to Hell, no doubt. That's the itinerary of most women, I believe. Get the brandy, boy, she'll be here presently.

ZACH. *(Backing away to* L.C.*)* No, I must stand guard till Father returns.

SALLY. *(At head of stairs)* Zach——

ZACH. Go to your room, Sally. (VAGABOND *rises.*)

SALLY. *(Comes downstairs, staring in wonderment at* VAGABOND*)* What does it mean?

ZACH. *(To* SALLY*)* Go to your room before Father returns.

VAGABOND. Oh, so this is Sally, the apple of your eye? Greetings, my good girl. You should be proud of your champion.

SALLY. *(Comes downstage a bit)* Who is this man?

VAGABOND. Congratulations, my boy. Hearty congratulations. I admire your good taste. Not so fair to gaze upon. No, not so fair to gaze upon, but what could be more beautiful than the gentleness and timidity of an innocent, ugly maid?

SALLY. Does the man call me ugly?

VAGABOND. *(Crosses and takes her hands)* Sally, there's a woman in distress. A gulp of brandy might save her life. Take the gun and hold me safe while he draws a glass. *(Drops her hands and turns to* ZACH*)* What say you, my boy? Come, 'tis for a woman I appeal.

SALLY. Where's the woman, Zach?

ZACH. In the shed—if there is one.

VAGABOND. *(Walks away)* Ha! He doubts my word, you see.

ZACH. *(To* SALLY*)* Father's gone to fetch her. Here—— *(He hands the pistol to* SALLY*)* Aim at his heart and shoot if he makes a move. (SALLY *points the gun at the* VAGABOND.*)* I'm not sure of the man. *(He backs to front of table* L.C.*)*

VAGABOND. *(At fireplace)* Crack me dead at the wink of an eye—it's my own request. Get the brandy, boy.

ZACH. *(Going up to door* L.*)* Be on the alert, Sally.

SALLY. I'll hold the man, go on. (ZACH *exits* L. SALLY *stands covering the* VAGABOND *with the pistol. The* VAGABOND *takes three steps toward* SALLY. *She backs three steps away from him, moving with him. He then backs three steps to* R. SALLY *advancing with him.*)

VAGABOND. *(Laughs as he moves to the fire)* Lower the gun, my girl, don't strain your nerves.

SALLY. No tricks—I'll shoot to kill.

VAGABOND. *(Amused)* Come, Sally, you're a better judge of character than Zach. A fair question: beneath this somewhat shabby exterior can you not trace something unmistakably refined and genteel?

SALLY. I don't care who you are, I'll shoot you down if you make a move.

VAGABOND. Bravo, my lass! *(Claps his hands)* By gad, such courage is a credit to your sex. *(Three KNOCKS on outside door* C.)

SALLY. Who's there?

FREEMAN. *(Off* C.) Unbolt the door.

SALLY. It's the Master.

VAGABOND. *(Starts up* C.) Shall I lift the bar?

SALLY. *(Goes up to door* C., *shifting the gun to her left hand)* Stay still, I'll attend to that.

VAGABOND. As you will, fair captor—'tis the natural politeness of my nature, nothing more. (SALLY *lifts the bar with her right hand, watching the* VAGABOND, *the pistol trained on him. The door swings open and* FREEMAN *enters—(CRASH)—carrying the apparently lifeless form of* VIOLET *in his arms.* SALLY *closes and bolts the door.* VAGABOND *goes quickly to* FREEMAN) Right here by the fire, sir. Right here, Mr. Landlord. I will take care of that, Mr. Landlord. Yes, right by the fire, sir. (VAGABOND *goes to* R. *of chair, kneels, takes* VIOLET'S *hand, which he pats.*)

FREEMAN. *(At L. of chair, takes off hat and great-coat, which he hands to SALLY, who has come down L. of him)* Where is my son?

SALLY. Gone for the brandy.

FREEMAN. And what are *you* doing downstairs?

SALLY. Keeping guard till Zach returns.

FREEMAN. That will do—go.

SALLY. Who's the woman, Master? *(Hands the pistol to FREEMAN.)*

FREEMAN. Never mind. Go. (SALLY *hangs* FREEMAN'S *coat on peg* R. *of door* C. *and goes upstairs, watching the* VAGABOND *and* VIOLET.)

VAGABOND. *(Still working over* VIOLET*)* And you doubted my every word. Did you find her in a faint?

FREEMAN. *(Crossing to fire)* Stretched over a log. I thought her dead at first.

VAGABOND. *(Chafing* VIOLET's *hands)* No, no. She's far from dead. The brandy will bring her to.

FREEMAN. I wonder who she is.

VAGABOND. What does it matter who she is? We know *what* she is.

FREEMAN. *What* is she?

VAGABOND. A woman.

FREEMAN. Have you ever seen her before?

VAGABOND. Once.

FREEMAN. Where?

VAGABOND. In the woodshed.

FREEMAN. I know that.

VAGABOND. Then why the question?

FREEMAN. Don't be facetious. Is she **your** friend?

VAGABOND. She's not my enemy, I hope.

FREEMAN. You play on words.

VAGABOND. *(Seriously)* I answer direct. Ask me if I've met her before tonight—if that's what you mean—and I'll say no. I never set eyes on this woman till she fired at you in self-defense. (VIOLET *moves slightly, beginning to regain consciousness. Impatiently)* My God, has the boy gone to *Spain* for the brandy?

FREEMAN. Hurry, Zach!

ZACH. *(Off L.)* I'm coming, Father. *(He enters from L. with a glass of brandy.* FREEMAN *takes glass from* ZACH. VAGABOND *takes glass from* FREEMAN.*)*

VAGABOND. That's my job, Mr. Landlord, if you please. My job, sir. My duty, Mr. Landlord. I'll take it, if you please, sir. There you are, you see. *(Goes to R. of armchair, kneels, moves glass to and fro underneath* VIOLET'S *nose.)*

FREEMAN. Why should she be out on a night like this? (VIOLET *stirs slightly.)*

VAGABOND. We'll soon know that. She's opening her eyes.

ZACH. *(*L.C., *staring at* VIOLET*)* Oh, then, the story of the woman was true!

VAGABOND. *(Arising)* Yes, my boy, stories of women are more apt to be true than the women of whom the stories are told. *(Going to R. of* VIOLET*)* Take a sip of this, my lass. The engine pumps more freely when the oil is squirted on. (FREEMAN *crosses to* C., *watching the* VAGABOND.*)*

ZACH. *(To* FREEMAN, *after a pause)* Who is she, have you learned?

FREEMAN. No, she's a riddle to me—so is the man.

VAGABOND. *(To* VIOLET, *as she sips some of the brandy)* That's the way! That's it! Take courage, plenty of courage; take courage. You'll need it for the inquisition you're about to face. *(Sarcastically. He places the brandy glass on mantelpiece. The* THREE MEN *stand watching* VIOLET *as she struggles back to consciousness.)*

VIOLET. *(At first stares blankly, then seemingly finds herself. She looks searchingly at the man, takes a sweeping glance around the room, then looks directly front)* In what part of God's world am I?

VAGABOND. What does it matter? It's *all* God's world.

VIOLET. *(To* VAGABOND*)* And who are you?

VAGABOND. I am one of God's creatures.

VIOLET. *(Indicating* ZACH *and* FREEMAN*)* And these two men—who are *they?*

VAGABOND. *(Shakes his head after a look at the* TWO MEN*)* Doubtless they'll answer for themselves. (VIOLET *looks at* FREEMAN.*)*

FREEMAN. *(To* VIOLET*)* My name is Freeman. I'm master here. *(Indicates* ZACH*)* This is my son.

VIOLET. I see. *(Looks front, puzzled)* And what am I doing here?

FREEMAN. Ah, that's what we'd like to know.

VIOLET. My mind isn't clear.

VAGABOND. Think back to the storm, my lass, and then perhaps you'll get your bearings.

VIOLET. The storm——! *(Leans forward as her memory slowly returns)* Yes, yes, the storm! *(Her face lights up as recollection comes to her.)*

VAGABOND. Show her the weapon, Freeman. Perhaps that may help.

FREEMAN. *(Crosses and shows* VIOLET *the pistol)* Ever see this before?

VIOLET. *(Recognizing the weapon, she reaches for it)* My pistol!

FREEMAN. *(Draws back quickly out of reach)* Ah, then it was *you* who fired the shot?

VIOLET. Fired a shot? *(Pause; then recollection returns)* Oh, yes, yes, I remember now. I ran to cover from the storm. I fell asleep and *dreamed* I was being shot at. I awoke with a start and fired at what seemed to be a ghost. (VAGABOND *gestures as though to say "You see."*) I was attacked from behind. (VAGABOND *points to himself.*) I tried to scream, but my throat went dry. (VAGABOND *points to his throat.)* My limbs sank from under me—and all went black.

VAGABOND. *(Pushes hands, palms downward, toward floor, then extends hands, palms up, as though to say, "You see." To* FREEMAN*)* Confirming the story I told, you see; and yet you doubted my every word.

FREEMAN. Wait. *(To* VIOLET*)* You say you ran to cover from the storm?

VIOLET. Yes, I remember now.

FREEMAN. Then what were you doing on the lonely road in the dead of night? Answer me that?

VIOLET. *(Looks at* FREEMAN, *then turns front)* The lonely road in the dead of night? I must think. *(Her mind is not clear. She is confused.)*

FREEMAN. Think fast and speak the truth. I'm not sure you're not in league with this man who begged the brandy.

VAGABOND. *(Laughing and singing)* "Ha, ha, ha —ha, ha, ha, ha, ha—ha, ha!"

VIOLET. *(To* VAGABOND*)* What does the man intimate?

VAGABOND. *(Laughs)* That we're a pair—that we're a pair, and that together we'd planned to rob the tavern of its golden plate and precious jewels. *(Laughs heartily)* There's a laugh in that for me. You've nothing but debts—— *(Laughs)* You said so yourself.

FREEMAN. *(Angrily)* Enough from you. *(To* VIOLET *after a pause)* Answer my question. Where were you bound for when the storm broke?

VIOLET. *(Leaning forward, her hands tightly grasping the arms of her chair)* Bound for? *(Thinking hard)* Oh, yes, yes, I remember now. I was on my way to the Capitol.

FREEMAN. To the Capitol! On foot?

VIOLET. On foot.

VAGABOND. Which proves she's not a horsethief, at least.

FREEMAN. *(Sarcastically, as he moves to* L. *of* ZACH*)* Huh! To the Capitol on foot! *(Turns to* VIOLET.*)*

ZACH. It can't be true, Father. It's fifty-two miles.

VIOLET. Fifty-two miles!

FREEMAN. From where do you hail?

VIOLET. Thirty miles south.

FREEMAN. Eighty-two miles.

ZACH. On foot.

FREEMAN. And why to the Capitol?

VIOLET. To see—the Governor.

FREEMAN. The Governor! You?

VIOLET. I.

FREEMAN. By appointment?

VIOLET. No—but to demand a hearing.

FREEMAN. *(Leaning over her)* What about? (VIOLET *cowers down in the chair.*) I must know. Answer my question. *(She cringes.)*

VIOLET. *(Turns to* VAGABOND. *Frightened)* Am I on trial for my life—or what does it mean?

VAGABOND. Why, the man's suspicious. Having trespassed on his property, naturally enough he wishes to satisfy himself that you did so with no dishonest purpose. Convince him if you can, but tell him only that which you feel he has the right to know. *(Looks over at* FREEMAN.*)*

FREEMAN. *(To* VIOLET, *after a look at the* VAGABOND*)* Answer me, woman! *(He yells the line.* VIOLET *cringes.)*

VAGABOND. Don't shout so, Freeman.

FREEMAN. Keep out of it, you! This is *my* roof over your head. *I* stand in judgment here.

VAGABOND. This is a tavern, not a court of law.

FREEMAN. I wish it were—that's where the case should be. Huh! Tramping to the Capitol, armed to the teeth and set to force herself upon the Governor. *(Goes to* VIOLET*)* Ha, an attempt at assassination! Aha!

VAGABOND. *(Amused)* Very well put together, cleverly thought out, beautifully dramatized, damned amusing. *(Laughs)* There's a laugh in it all for me, Freeman.

FREEMAN. Take care. I'm not a man to be laughed at.

ZACH. *(Warningly)* Be careful, Father.

FREEMAN. *(To* ZACH*)* Be quiet, you.

VIOLET. *(To* VAGABOND*)* Why does the man say such things? (FREEMAN *turns to* ZACH, *undecided what to do.* ZACH *pantomimes to his father to be careful, then crosses* R. *of table* L.C.*)*

FREEMAN. *(Moves up* C., *keeping his eye on* VIOLET *and* VAGABOND*)* Neither one of you leaves this tavern until I have satisfactory accounts of you both.

VAGABOND. What? *(Crossing to* FREEMAN*)* Come, come, it's creeping on to midnight. The woman is footsore, weary and dazed. In God's name, be human. Offer her a place to sleep and a bit to eat.

FREEMAN. And who's to pay for these accommodations?

VAGABOND. I beg pardon?

FREEMAN. I ask, who's to pay for these accommodations?

VAGABOND. *(To* VIOLET*)* Have you the money, Miss? *(She makes no reply. He turns to* FREEMAN*)* Come, Freeman. Now surely the weapon in your hand is well worth the price of lodging and a crust of bread. *(Pause, then he goes to* VIOLET, *pats her hands comfortingly, his eyes fixed on* FREEMAN. FREEMAN *stands looking at pistol in his hands, undecided what to do.)*

ZACH. *(After a pause he calls to his father)*

Father. (FREEMAN *gives the* VAGABOND *a look, then goes* L., *followed by* VAGABOND. *As* FREEMAN *turns on him, the* VAGABOND *goes back to* VIOLET *and takes her hands in his.* FREEMAN *goes* R. *of table* L.C. *Aside*) It's the best way. Have Sally watch the woman's room while I guard the man. Willum can get the sheriff. (FREEMAN *thinks a second, takes a good look at the* VAGABOND, *suddenly decides on his course of action, and moves to the stairs.* VAGABOND *pats* VIOLET'S *hand.*)

FREEMAN. (*Calling upstairs*) Sally! (*He comes down* C. ZACH *rises.*)

SALLY. (*Appearing at head of stairs*) Yes, Master?

FREEMAN. (*As* SALLY *comes down to* R. *of him*) This woman goes to the cot in Number Three.

SALLY. Yes, Master. (ZACH *goes above table* L.C.)

FREEMAN. Serve tea and bread if she asks for food.

SALLY. (*Moving up to* R. *side of stairs*) Yes, Master.

VAGABOND. (*Goes to* FREEMAN) Bravo, friend Freeman. May you live a thousand years. More power to you, my friend. (VIOLET *rises, tries to get to fire, but staggers.* VAGABOND *crosses quickly to* VIOLET) Let me assist you, Miss. (*Puts his hand out to steady her.*)

VIOLET. (*Going to fireplace*) I'm all right, thank you. I'm quite myself. I—— (*She sways and falls in a dead faint in* VAGABOND'S *arms.* SALLY *screams.*)

FREEMAN. (*To* SALLY) Be quiet, you fool!

ZACH. (*Rushes to* VIOLET, *picks her up in his arms and stands motionless momentarily, shouting meanwhile*) I'll take her, sir. I'll take her, sir.

VAGABOND. Take her, my boy. Take her, my boy.

FREEMAN. Number Three, Son. Number Three. The cot in Number Three. Hurry up, my boy.

ZACH. I understand, Father. I understand. (ZACH *goes to first landing with* VIOLET *in his arms.* SALLY *stands at the newel post.* FREEMAN C. *stage.* VAGABOND *at* L. *of armchair, pointing upward.*)

VAGABOND. At last, at last my dream's come true. All my life I've longed to be a hero. First I save the landlord's life and now I see the deserted maiden placed upon her downy couch where she may dream her dreams of vengeance sweet. *(Crosses to foot of stairs)* By gad, what a night. It's a story book night for me. *(CRASH.)* What a storm! What a glorious storm! What a damn fool any man is to be indoors on a night like this. *(CRASH.)* Lead on, my boy. Oh, what a night! What a storm! Lead on, my boy. (ZACH *and* VAGABOND *exit upstairs.*)

FREEMAN. Sally—— (SALLY *goes to* R. *of him.*) Listen to me, my girl. Sleep at the woman's door. If she makes a move to escape, scream and warn the house. Do you understand? *(Crosses to window.)*

SALLY. Yes, Master. Shall I make the tea?

FREEMAN. Don't waste the stuff. She may sleep through the night without waking. *(Crosses* R. *to fireplace.)*

SALLY. *(Going toward the stairs)* Very well, Master.

WILLUM. *(Appearing at head of stairs)* Zach said you wanted me, Master Freeman. Is it true, or is he making game of me again?

FREEMAN. *(Looking front)* Hurry, Willum, be quick!

WILLUM. *(Runs down to foot of stairs)* Yes, Master. *(Pinches* SALLY's *cheek)* Ah, my little darling!

SALLY. *(Slaps* WILLUM's *face)* Keep your hands off me.

WILLUM. *(Nursing his cheek)* Rotten little spitfire.

SALLY. Idiot! *(She runs upstairs and off.)*

WILLUM. *(Down to R. of FREEMAN, holding his cheek)* Did you see what she did, Master?

FREEMAN. Shut up and listen to me! Get to the barn, stride the mare and ride as fast as God will let you to the Sheriff's house. Tell him we've made a round-up and to rush here without delay.

(THUNDER.)

WILLUM. *(Goes upstage, then comes back to FREEMAN)* Ride through a storm like this!

FREEMAN. It's the *Master* speaking. Do as I say.

(LIGHTNING.)

WILLUM. Yes, Master. *(Goes up C., then back to FREEMAN)* If the mare is struck by lightning, don't blame me. *(Again goes up C. and again comes back)* What do you want the Sheriff for?

FREEMAN. Shut up, you fool, and go get him.

WILLUM. Yes, Master. *(As he goes up to pegs and puts on overcoat)* What sort of a night is this, anyway? Thunder, lightning, shootin', screamin'— *(Puts on his hat and comes down to FREEMAN)* And tell me, Master, who's the faintin' woman and the stranger I passed in the hall? Why are they in the tavern? When did they come?

FREEMAN. Damn you for your questions! Hurry, I say.

WILLUM. *(Buttoning coat)* Keep that stranger away from Sally, that's all I ask. I love that gal and I'll kill any man that tries to come between us.

FREEMAN. *(Yells)* Shut up and go, you fool!

(CRASH.)

WILLUM. *(Goes to window)* No man can ride through a storm like this.

FREEMAN. You can and must.

WILLUM. *(His hand on doorknob)* If you don't care for my life, think of the horse.

FREEMAN. *(Strides upstage in a rage.* WILLUM *opens door)* To hell with the horse! Go, I say! *(CRASH.) (He pushes* WILLUM *out* C., *closes and bars the door and comes down in front of table* L.C., *facing front. The* VAGABOND *and* ZACH *enter downstairs.* ZACH *crosses* R.*)*

(Rolling of THUNDER until VAGABOND *comes.)*

VAGABOND. *(Down to* FREEMAN*)* Friend Freeman, to my mind the ceremony of shaking hands has always been more or less of an asinine idea, but I can think of no other way of expressing my thanks for your generous action toward the woman upstairs—and so I bend to custom—I bend to custom. *(Bows and extends his hand)* Your hand, sir.

FREEMAN. *(Pause. He makes no move to take hand)* I must always know with whom I'm shaking hands. What's your name?

VAGABOND. My name? Well, if I knew I'd tell you. That's fair enough, I hope.

FREEMAN. Who *are* you?

VAGABOND. I've been trying to find that out for years.

FREEMAN. Are you a fool, or do you think me one?

VAGABOND. If I were fool enough to say I thought you a fool, you'd think me a fool for saying it. *(Again offers his hand)* You still refuse to shake my hand?

FREEMAN. No, I refuse to allow you to shake mine.

VAGABOND. *(Laughs)* Cutting, but well put. Whether you believe it or not, I still have my first man's hand to shake. Thank God, my record's clean.

FREEMAN. And so is my hand.

VAGABOND. *(Laughs)* A dirty dig, but clever— damned clever. *(Pokes* FREEMAN *in the ribs, laughs, looks around, thinks, decides to act, and starts up* R.*)* Well, there's nothing to keep me here, nothing more, so I think I'll bid you both goodnight. *(Picks up hat, cloak and staff and prepares to go.)*

FREEMAN. *(R. of table, raises his gun as VAGABOND starts up C.)* Stop! Another step and you're a dead man.

VAGABOND. And am I to understand that I'm to be detained?

FREEMAN. You're my prisoner, Mr. Stranger.

VAGABOND. Yes? And might I ask with what authority you make that statement?

FREEMAN. This weapon authorizes me to speak. You don't leave here until I know why you came and who you are.

VAGABOND. *(Putting hat, cloak and staff on table up R.)* So be it. *(Coming down C.)* But, if I'm to be denied the privilege of the great outdoors and the beauties of the storm, I demand refreshment. Come, I'm famished. What say you, Mr. Jailer? *(He comes to R. of table. ZACH L. of table. FREEMAN laughs.)* He laughs! He laughs! 'Tis an encouraging sign, I hope.

FREEMAN. *(Laughing)* I'm laughing at your monumental nerve. Egotism 'tis thy name.

VAGABOND. You're going to like me after all, and you'll admire me later on. I was sure you had a sense of humor. Let's get properly acquainted, eh? *(Mocks FREEMAN's laughter)* Bring on the food while the landlord laughs. A biscuit and a mug of beer and I'll tell you the tale of a fool's career. Come, stand treat this once and I'll ask nothing more than a pipe and tobacco leaf to top it off. What say you, Mr. Jailer?

FREEMAN. Zach!

ZACH. Yes, Father.

FREEMAN. Fetch the beggar the order he gave.

ZACH. Yes, Father. *(Goes out L.)*

VAGABOND. Aha! Again I proclaim you a most generous gentleman.

FREEMAN. *(After a pause)* Sit down. *(He sits L. of table L.C.)*

VAGABOND. *(Sits at table, opposite FREEMAN)* You see now we're as thick as thieves. I knew it. I was sure we'd be friends before the night was over. *(Leans back comfortably in his chair.)*

FREEMAN. Well, proceed—I'm anxious to hear.

VAGABOND. Hear what?

FREEMAN. The story of your life.

VAGABOND. The story of *my* life?

FREEMAN. Was not that the agreement? In exchange for the biscuit and the mug of beer you're to tell me the tale of a fool's career. 'Twas your own suggestion.

VAGABOND. No, no. No, you misunderstood, my friend. 'Twas not to myself I referred—'tis of another fool I would tell—another fool. Shall I begin? *(Pause)* Once upon a time—a long time ago——

FREEMAN. *(Rises in anger, bangs the table and yells)* Stop! I've heard enough. *(Calls)* Zach!

ZACH. *(Enters from L. and comes above table, L.C.)* Coming, Father.

FREEMAN. No food or drink—the man's a trickster.

VAGABOND. Choose your words, Freeman.

FREEMAN. I repeat, you're a trickster. You're worse than that. You're a blackguard.

VAGABOND. You're a liar—I'm not.

FREEMAN. *(Pointing his pistol at VAGABOND)* Take that back.

VAGABOND. I'm damned if I will.

FREEMAN. *(Leans over table, pointing pistol)* Take that back or I'll kill you.

VAGABOND. You're a liar, you won't. You haven't the nerve of a child. I *dare* you to shoot.

FREEMAN. *(Taken aback)* You're a brave man whoever you are.

VAGABOND. Well, not necessarily brave, for I

happened to know that the gun was empty, you see. I saw to that before I tossed it to you when I disarmed myself a while ago. (FREEMAN *laughs.*) I was sure it would amuse you. (FREEMAN *opens chamber of gun and finds it empty.* BOTH MEN *laugh.*) Damned silly, my pretended bravado, but I loved the drama of the thing. Really, I loved the drama of the thing even though 'twas only make-believe. Come, rescind that cancellation. Bring on the banquet and when I've finished I'll entertain you till you roar. By gad, sir, I'll do a trick with cards that will amaze you, or perhaps you would rather—I'd dance—— (*Crosses* C., *does a few steps and returns to chair*) Or perhaps you would rather I should sing. More of my accomplishments. My repertoire of ballads is well worth the hearing. (*Sings*)
"As big as a cow, as tame as a calf,
  She settles the problems of life with a laugh."
Chuh-chuh-chuh, chuh-chuh-chuh-chuh.

(*The* TWO MEN *laugh uproariously. The* GOVERNOR *KNOCKS on door* C. ALL *listening.* FREEMAN *crosses* C., *pocketing gun. Another* KNOCK. VAGABOND *rises, crosses* L. *a few paces, wheels, faces door; motions* FREEMAN *to open door.* FREEMAN *indignant.*)

GOVERNOR. (*Off* C.) Open the door!
FREEMAN. (*After a pause*) Who would enter?
GOVERNOR. (*Commandingly*) Open the door.

(FREEMAN *opens the door.* GOVERNOR LAMSON, MRS. LAMSON, VIRGINIA *and* TOM ALLEN *enter.*) (*CRASH.*)
(*Come down stage in line, and stand motionless. There is a few moments' silence as* ALL *stand looking around the room, then* VIRGINIA *no-*

tices the fire and calls her mother's attention to it. The TWO WOMEN *cross to fireplace, the* VAGABOND *moving toward* VIRGINIA *as she crosses.* FREEMAN *remains at door, which he has barred.* VAGABOND *crosses to front of table* L.C., *facing front.)*

(The WOMEN *remove their outer wraps.* ALLEN *puts his hat and cloak on table up* R., *then comes down to* VIRGINIA *and puts her cape on chair* R. *of fireplace. The* GOVERNOR *stands watching the* VAGABOND. *After a pause the* GOVERNOR *crosses and puts his hat on chair up* R.; *takes off his cloak, folds it and places it on* L. *bannister and comes down* C. *After eyeing the* VAGABOND *closely for a few seconds, the* GOVERNOR *goes to his wife and daughter at fireplace, puts his arms about them and talks to them in undertones, then returns to* C. *stage.)* (CRASH.)

(ZACH *watches* VAGABOND *intently.* VAGABOND *turns quickly to* ZACH, *and* ZACH *jumps back, frightened.)*

GOVERNOR. *(After a pause he turns to* FREEMAN *and* VAGABOND*)* Which of you is the landlord? (VAGABOND *moves to* L. *and upstage.)*

FREEMAN. *(Crosses to* GOVERNOR*)* Right here, sir; at your service.

GOVERNOR. I am Governor Lamson.

FREEMAN. *(Astonished)* Governor Lamson! *(Bowing)* Your Excellency! (VAGABOND *becomes interested.)*

GOVERNOR. *(Turns to* VAGABOND*)* My wife and daughter, gentlemen. *(The introduction is acknowledged)* And my daughter's intended husband, Mr. Tom Allen.

ALLEN. *(Haughtily)* How do you do, gentlemen? *(The* THREE MEN *bow.* VAGABOND *saunters up and down stage, flirting with* VIRGINIA.*)*

GOVERNOR. We must lodge here, landlord. Can you take care of us for the night?

FREEMAN. *(Bowing low)* An honor, Your Excellency. (MRS. LAMSON *sits in armchair at fireplace.*)

GOVERNOR. My coach is in the yard. Your stable is locked. Will you have your men see that my horses are well cared for and that my driver finds a place to sleep?

FREEMAN. *(Bowing low)* At once, Your Excellency. *(Calls to* ZACH *as he goes up)* Zach——

ZACH. *(Going up* C. *The* GOVERNOR *crosses to fireplace)* I understand, Father. *(He picks up lantern and puts on overcoat.)*

ALLEN. *(To* ZACH*)* And boy, the luggage. (FREEMAN *unbars and opens door for* ZACH.)

ZACH. Yes, sir. *(He goes out* C.*)* *(CRASH.)* (FREEMAN *closes and bars door; comes downstage to* GOVERNOR.)

GOVERNOR. Oh, landlord.

FREEMAN. *(Coming down* C.*)* Yes, Your Excellency.

GOVERNOR. Hot toddies, quickly, we're perished.

FREEMAN. *(Bowing)* Hot toddies at once, Your Excellency. *(Bows again, looks at* VAGABOND *and exits* L.*)*

(There is a pause. The GOVERNOR *removes coat, pats his wife's hand, then goes upstage, eyeing* VAGABOND. VIRGINIA *goes to her mother, talks a moment in undertones, then returns to fire. The* GOVERNOR *looks up the stairs, then at* VAGABOND. ALLEN *crosses to* GOVERNOR, *touches him on arm. As the* GOVERNOR *turns,* ALLEN *whispers to him. When the* GOVERNOR *shakes his head,* ALLEN *returns to fire above* VIRGINIA.*)*

GOVERNOR. A bad storm, young man.

VAGABOND. Huh?

GOVERNOR. A bad storm.

VAGABOND. *(Rises)* Oh, no, a good storm; as glorious a storm as I've ever seen. *(Sits again on table, looking front.* ALL *turn and watch him.)*

GOVERNOR. *(After a look at his wife and daughter)* Well, that's one way of looking at it, I dare say. *(Eyeing the* VAGABOND, *he moves up* C. *and then down to his wife.)*

MRS. LAMSON. *(Seated* R.*)* Are your nerves still on edge, Robert, or have you quieted down?

GOVERNOR. *(Patting her hand)* I'm all right, perfectly all right, dear. *(He goes up* C.*)*

ALLEN. *(Crosses upstage)* Come over and get warm, Governor.

VIRGINIA. Yes, do, please, Dad. It's a wonderful fire.

VAGABOND. It is indeed. It is indeed—a *most* wonderful fire. But another log will make it even more so. *(Bowing low to* VIRGINIA*)* With your permission, Miss Virginia. *(Takes mincing steps* R., *picks up log, exhibits it, puts on fire; kneels, places log, rises, bows, minces* L. *to table* L.C.; *faces front; strikes attitude.)*

VIRGINIA. Oh, thank you so much. *(Sits down)* There's something so perfectly romantic about a log fire, don't you think so, Tom? *(She looks at* VAGABOND *as she says this.* VAGABOND *returns* VIRGINIA'S *look, then glances over at* ALLEN, *who is glaring at him.)*

ALLEN. *(To* VIRGINIA*)* If *you* do, dear. Are you still frightened?

VIRGINIA. Not a bit now. How are you feeling, Dad?

GOVERNOR. *(Going to* L. *of* MRS. LAMSON*)* My nervousness is gone. I'm worried about your mother now.

Mrs. Lamson. Don't worry about me, dear. I'm as right as rain.

Virginia. Don't mention rain, Mother, after what we've been through. (All *"ssh" heavily.*)

Governor. Remember, Tom, there must be no publicity given to this affair. (*Goes up* c.)

Allen. With election coming on? I understand your position. (*Crosses* l.) Governor, not a word out of me. (*The* Governor *paces moodily up and down stage.*)

Mrs. Lamson. Take it easy, Robert. Do please sit down and rest.

Governor. (*Coming down to* l. *of his wife*) All right, dear, if it will please you I'll sit down and rest. (*Sits* r. *of his wife.*) (CRASH.)

Mrs. Lamson. That's better, dear. (Violet *is heard screaming from upstairs. There is a startled pause, then* All *rise.*)

Virginia. What was that?

Sally. (*Runs on from upstairs, calling excitedly*) Master! Master Freeman!

Vagabond. (*Crosses to* Sally) What is it, Sally, what's wrong?

Sally. The sick woman—she jumped out of bed. She's afraid of the storm!

Vagabond. Quiet her down, Sally; you know how to do it.

Sally. I'll try, sir. (*She looks in surprise at the strangers and exits upstairs.*)

Mrs. Lamson. (*Crosses to* Vagabond) Is someone ill?

Vagabond. (*Comes down a step*) Yes, a stranger. A stranger driven in by the storm.

Virginia. (*Over to the* Vagabond) A woman?

Vagabond. A woman. She's very tired, very weak.

Governor. Too bad. Perhaps you could help her, dear.

MRS. LAMSON. I'd be only too glad.

VAGABOND. No, no. *(Halts* MRS. LAMSON*)* She needs rest more than attention—rest more than attention—rest more than attention. *(There is a pause.* MRS. LAMSON *comes down above armchair* R. VAGABOND *moves upstage; looks upstage; looks upstairs; comes downstage and looks at* VIRGINIA, *who turns away.)*

ALLEN. Virginia.

VAGABOND. Well, Governor. On your way to the Capitol?

GOVERNOR. Yes, left Burtonville at seven o'clock. We should have been in the mansion an hour ago.

VAGABOND. You were held up by the storm, I suppose?

GOVERNOR. Yes, held up by the storm. *(Looks warningly at* ALLEN.*)*

VIRGINIA. Yes, *held up.* Lord—— *(*ALL *"ssh."*)* What an experience!

MRS. LAMSON. Hush, dear; you heard what your father said, a while ago. (VAGABOND *moves over to table* L.C.)

VIRGINIA. I'm sorry, Dad, I—— *(Stops short as* VAGABOND *looks at her.)*

(VAGABOND *moves around to* L. *upper corner of table as* FREEMAN *enters from* L. *with a trayful of toddies. As he passes* VAGABOND *he gives him a sour look.* FREEMAN *passes tray first to* MRS. LAMSON, *who declines with a shake of her head, then to the* GOVERNOR.)

FREEMAN. *(As he serves* GOVERNOR*)* Here you are, Your Excellency. I'm so sorry to have kept you waiting.

GOVERNOR. *(Taking a toddy from the tray)* Not at all, landlord. Quick service, I should say.

FREEMAN. *(Passing tray to* ALLEN, *who helps*

himself) My man is out. I mixed them myself. I hope they're good. *(Goes to* C.*)*

VIRGINIA. *(Crosses and takes a glass from tray)* Anything hot is good right now no matter how it tastes.

FREEMAN. *(To* MRS. LAMSON*)* Can't I persuade you?

MRS. LAMSON. No, thanks; not for me.

GOVERNOR. *(Crosses to* VAGABOND*)* Won't you join us, young man? My wife does not imbibe. (FREEMAN *scowls at* VAGABOND.)

VAGABOND. *(With a low bow)* It would be an honor, Governor—(GOVERNOR *gives office to* FREEMAN.*)*—a great honor. Though seldom does liquor pass my lips, I can hardly refuse the chance to drink a toast to Governor Lamson, his most helpful wife, and his extremely charming daughter. *(He bows to* GOVERNOR *and* LADIES *in turn, then orders* FREEMAN *to him with the stamp of his foot and the snap of his fingers.* FREEMAN *crosses unwillingly and presents the tray to the* VAGABOND, *who picks up a spoon; stirs the toddy; drops the spoon on the tray with a great clatter; picks up his drink and nods a dismissal to* FREEMAN, *who moves down to* L. *of table. The* VAGABOND *raises his glass for a toast. The* OTHERS *also raise their glasses. Holds glass aloft)* To Governor Lamson! May the rogue who held up your coach between Burtonville and here come to no good, and within the year. Divine, delicious, superb nectar of the gods. (ALL *drink. Crosses up* C.; *puts glass on tray on* R. *table.)*

FREEMAN. *(Drops the tray on the* L.C. *table in his astonishment)* Held up by a highwayman, Your Excellency!

ALLEN. *(To* VAGABOND *as he comes down* R.*)* How did *you* know that?

GOVERNOR. Yes, how did you know that?

VAGABOND. Come, Governor, come. I'd be a poor

hand at word gathering if I failed to guess what Miss Virginia meant a while ago when she laid so much significance upon the words "held up." (FREEMAN *crosses to* GOVERNOR.)

MRS. LAMSON. Virginia, I warned you.

GOVERNOR. Gentlemen, not a word of this. I swear you both to secrecy.

FREEMAN. *(Raising his right hand)* I take a solemn oath, Your Excellency.

GOVERNOR. *(To* VAGABOND*)* And you, young man?

VAGABOND. My word is all I have—I give it.

FREEMAN. *(After a suspicious look at* VAGABOND*)* Where did it happen, Your Excellency, and how long ago?

GOVERNOR. Less than half an hour ago, a few miles south, just as we were turning off the pike. The driver tried to speed up the horses, but——

ALLEN. Why discuss it with these men, Governor? *(Takes glass from* VIRGINIA*)* They've pledged themselves to silence, that's enough.

GOVERNOR. You're right, Tom; we'll forget the matter. Gentlemen, you've given your word.

ALLEN. *(Puts* VIRGINIA'S *glass on mantel)* Come, come, gentlemen, it's late. We'll retire if you'll show us to our quarters.

GOVERNOR. Yes, we must be on our way by early morn. *(Hands his glass to* ALLEN, *who puts it on mantel.)*

FREEMAN. *(Crossing to stairs, bowing low)* Right this way, Your Excellency. (VAGABOND *goes below table* L.C.*)* There are plenty of rooms to choose from at this time of the year. I'll have my wench, Sally, take good care of the ladies. Follow me, please, Your Excellency, follow me. (FREEMAN *remains on upper landing. The* GOVERNOR *goes upstage, gets his hat and cloak, stands aside and allows his wife to pass on up the steps. She re-*

mains on landing. ALLEN *stays below the fireplace.*
VAGABOND *at C. stage.* VIRGINIA *follows her mother.*
VAGABOND *meanwhile flirts with* VIRGINIA. GOVERNOR *sees him and shoots him indignant look.)*

GOVERNOR. *(At L. of newel post, to* VAGABOND*)*
Goodnight, young man.

VAGABOND. Goodnight, Governor, goodnight, and good luck to you always. *(Crosses over L.)* May your re-election, which I predict, make you as happy as this meeting has made me tonight; this meeting with Governor Lamson, his most helpful wife, and his extremely charming daughter. *(He makes the* THREE *a sweeping bow. The* GOVERNOR *crosses to* MRS. LAMSON.*)*

VIRGINIA. *(Goes up the stairs, stops on the third step and turns to the* VAGABOND. *To* ALLEN, *as she looks down at* VAGABOND*)* Isn't he the quaintest man you ever met? *(*VAGABOND *smiles at her, advances and bows.)*

ALLEN. *(Impatiently)* Yes, yes! Go along, Virginia.

VIRGINIA. *(To* VAGABOND*)* Goodnight.

VAGABOND. *(Advances few paces)* Goodnight, Miss Virginia. Sweet dreams to you tonight, tomorrow night, and ten thousand nights to come.

VIRGINIA. Goodnight.

ALLEN. *(After a scowling look at* VAGABOND*)*
Go along, Virginia. *(*GOVERNOR *and* MRS. LAMSON *go upstairs, followed by* VIRGINIA *and* ALLEN. VIRGINIA *turns and smiles down at* VAGABOND *before she exits at head of stairs.)*

VAGABOND. Goodnight, Miss Virginia; goodnight, Miss Virginia. *(Stands watching them off, then turns front, smiling delightedly. After a moment he goes upstage, peers through the window, then comes down to C., giving an imitation of the manners and speech of the other characters)* "I mixed them myself, Your Excellency." "I take a solemn oath, your Excellency." "Right this way, your Excellency." "Why discuss it with these gentlemen, Governor? They've pledged themselves to silence, that's enough." *(Sings)*

As big as a cow, but as tame as a calf,
She settles the problems of life with a laugh.

"Isn't he the quaintest man you ever met?" *(He looks toward stairs, goes up to* L. *of them, and stands looking pensively off in the direction* VIRGINIA *has gone. Comes downstage)* "Isn't he the quaintest man you ever met?" (ZACH *KNOCKS on the* C. *door. The* VAGABOND *drops to knee, listens intently, unbars and opens door just a crack to see who it is, then opens it wide and admits* ZACH —(CRASH)—*who enters with the travellers' luggage. He does not see* VAGABOND, *who has moved back of door.* ZACH *puts luggage down* R.C. *and hangs his coat and hat on the peg on the landing. As he turns to come down he sees* VAGABOND *for the first time and stands staring at him in astonishment, surprised to find the man alone and unguarded. He comes downstage about chair* R.) Ah, Zach, my lad, and did you put the knighted coachman to bed?

ZACH. He's all right; he's comfortable. Where's father?

VAGABOND. *(Going to newel post on stairs)* Showing his celebrated guests to their various chambers.

ZACH. And left you here alone—unguarded?

VAGABOND. Alone and unguarded. And do you suppose I'd run away—run away and try to escape from what I've just seen? No, my lad, the royal horses you just stabled could not drag me from this spot. Not till I get another look at Virginia will I stray one inch from the tavern. *(Stands, looking upstairs.)*

ZACH. You've no right to say such things about **His Excellency's** daughter. Besides, she's engaged.

VAGABOND. *(Coming down* C. *Takes* ZACH *by hand)* Ah, but the engagement is going to be broken off.

ZACH. When?

VAGABOND. In the morning.

ZACH. What do you mean?

VAGABOND. It must be splendid to be engaged, eh, Zach?

ZACH. *(Dreamily)* Yes, it must be.

VAGABOND. You're really in love with Sally, aren't you, Zach?

ZACH. *(On the defensive)* What if I am?

VAGABOND. Supposing—suppose your father should give his consent?

ZACH. Oh, there's no chance of that.

VAGABOND. You're wrong. There is—and he will.

ZACH. When?

VAGABOND. *(Slight pause)* In the morning.

ZACH. Why should all these things happen in the morning?

VAGABOND. Wait and see. *(Goes* L.*)* Wait and see.

ZACH. *(Pause)* What kind of a man *are* you?

VAGABOND. Would you really like to know, Zach?

ZACH. I would.

VAGABOND. Then I'll tell you. *(Takes* ZACH *by hand. Down* C. *stage)* But not now, not now—in the morning. *(Goes to position at newel post, looks upstairs)* Virginia—Virginia—— *(Prances a bit and sings)*

As big as a cow and as tame as a calf.

She settles the problems of life with a laugh.

(He goes to L. *of* L.C. *table, places chair; admonishes* ZACH *to be silent, yawns, stretches, places both feet on table; puts lips to fingers to warn* ZACH *to be silent, closes his eyes and is ostensibly asleep.)*

(ZACH *watches him closely for a while, takes two*

*grips in his hands, cautiously backs away.
FREEMAN comes downstairs, motions* ZACH *to
take bags away.* ZACH *exits upstairs.* FREE-
MAN *comes down to* VAGABOND, *peers at him,
thinks, makes a decision, lights lamp. Sees*
ZACH *coming downstairs and calls him over to
armchair in which he sits.* ZACH *kneels at his
R.)*

FREEMAN. Take the lantern and wait on the road for Willum; head him off and tell him to hide the Sheriff in the barn.

ZACH. Hide the Sheriff in the barn? Why, Father? *(Warn CURTAIN.)*

FREEMAN. I can't bring him into the tavern until the Governor goes.

ZACH. When is he going?

FREEMAN. In the morning.

ZACH. But, Father, must I wait in the road in a storm like this?

FREEMAN. It's your father speaking.

ZACH. Yes, Father. (ZACH *puts on his hat and coat as* FREEMAN *goes to* C. *door.* ZACH *lights lantern and exits, his father opening the door for him.)*
(CRASH.)

FREEMAN. *(Closes and bars door, comes down to the sleeping* VAGABOND, *shakes him by the foot to waken him)* Come, stranger, I'll show you where you're going to sleep.

VAGABOND. Oh, am I to sleep? Well, I had no idea of sleeping—— Tired, weary, exhausted, driven from the roads by the downpour of the rain and the sting of the hail. Drenched to the skin and trembling with fear and cold. However, I had no idea of sleeping, but—but—if you insist. (VAGA-
BOND *sings couplet as he rises to his feet)*

As big as a cow and as tame as a calf,
She settles the problems of life with a laugh.

FREEMAN. *(Backing away from him, putting fingers to lips, admonishing* VAGABOND *to be silent)* Hush, you'll wake the Governor.

VAGABOND. Oh, is he asleep already? *(CRASH.)* Ha, ha. Well, if he was, he isn't. (FREEMAN *backing to stairs, admonishing* VAGABOND *to be quiet.)*

VAGABOND. "After you, Your Excellency." *(Mocks* FREEMAN.*)*   *(CRASH.)*

FREEMAN. Hush, hush, hush.

(When VAGABOND *reaches the third step on first landing another crash is heard.)*   *(CRASH.)*

*(*VAGABOND *looks toward Heaven, puts finger to lips and raises them toward ceiling three times, exits slowly upstairs. CRASHES continue until Curtain is down.)*

CURTAIN

ACT TWO

SCENE: *Same as Act I.*

TIME: *An hour or two later.*

AT RISE: *Stage is bare. The LIGHTING is the same as at the end of Act I. The door is barred.*
About ten seconds before rising of Curtain, THUNDER is heard. Continues quite hard until VAGABOND reaches point behind VIRGINIA in armchair. Whenever VAGABOND looks out window, LIGHTNING flashes.
After a pause, the VAGABOND enters on the stairs. He comes to the landing, looks down into the room, then back in the direction of the sleeping rooms. After making sure that the room below is vacant he descends on tiptoe. Arriving at the foot of the stairs he takes a sweeping glance about the room, then goes to window up L., *and peers out into the storm. At the sound of a footstep he turns quickly toward the stairs. Opens the door, peers out, returns to* C. *of room, then to window, then exits to room off* L., *closing the door.*
A slight pause, and then VIRGINIA enters on stairs. She comes to landing, looks over the bannister and down into the room to see if she is alone, turns and looks at door up C. *and window.)* (CRASH.)

Draws back, affrighted. Hurries to the big armchair, where she snuggles comfortably.

After a short pause, the VAGABOND *enters quietly from* L., *watches* VIRGINIA *a moment, then goes above the chair in which she is seated.*

VAGABOND. *(Softly, almost in a whisper)* Comfortable, Miss Virginia?

VIRGINIA. *(Startled, she turns in the direction of the voice)* Who's that? *(Arises.)*

VAGABOND. Hush! Hush! Don't wake the Governor. With important duties of State to perform, his slumbers must not be disturbed.

VIRGINIA. *(With a smile of recognition)* Oh, it's you!

VAGABOND. 'Tis I—just as you expected.

VIRGINIA. Why—I thought I was alone.

VAGABOND. You are—unquestionably alone—in a class by yourself. Your individuality is absolutely pronounced. *(As* VIRGINIA *starts to answer, the* VAGABOND *puts his finger to his lips in warning, goes to foot of stairs, looks up and around, then comes down stage, gets the chair from* R. *of table* L.C. *and sits* L. *of* VIRGINIA. VIRGINIA *also sits.)*

VIRGINIA. *(Slight pause; she laughs lightly)* You're about the quaintest man I ever met.

VAGABOND. You said that once before tonight.

VIRGINIA. I meant it.

VAGABOND. I was sure you did.

VIRGINIA. You're terribly—cute.

VAGABOND. Cute?

VIRGINIA. Interesting, I mean.

VAGABOND. Oh! Then say what you mean, my lass. You speak paradoxically. Never yet have I seen anything cute that was interesting, or anything interesting that was cute.

VIRGINIA. *(Laughing)* I must try to remember that.

VAGABOND. Do. Try also to remember who said it, will you?

VIRGINIA. And why?

VAGABOND. Because I should love to have you like me. (VIRGINIA *shows confusion.*) That doesn't mean that I'd like to have you love me. No, I should not care for that, for while I like you very much— oh, very much— I swear to you that I do not love you.

VIRGINIA. *(Laughing)* You marvelous person, you. *(Leans toward him, amused)* Then you *admit* that you like me—just a little.

VAGABOND. Just a little—just a little bit more than any other girl I've ever met. But that does not mean so much—for I do not like women as a rule.

VIRGINIA. *(Laughs. Looking toward fire)* No?

VAGABOND. No. *(Looking into the fire)* There's something so perfectly romantic about a log fire, don't you think so?

VIRGINIA. *(Amused)* Ah, you remember things that are said, too, don't you?

VAGABOND. Oh, yes, especially when impressed by those who say them.

VIRGINIA. *(Laughs)* Be careful—I'm engaged.

VAGABOND. I'm always careful—at least careful enough not to have become engaged.

VIRGINIA. You're skeptical.

VAGABOND. Skeptical? No, practical.

VIRGINIA. *(Laughs heartily, but quietly)* You're very amusing. *(The* VAGABOND *bows.)* Who are you?

VAGABOND. What does it matter who I am so long as I amuse you?

VIRGINIA. At least give me your name.

VAGABOND. A thousand names if you like: John, James, Jeremiah, Tom, Dick or Harry—what does it matter? Such a label will not transform me into what I'm not.

VIRGINIA. And what is it you're not?

VAGABOND. Not what you think I am.

VIRGINIA. And what do you think I think you are?

VAGABOND. *(Slight pause)* An enigma.

VIRGINIA. *(Laughs)* A splendid guess.

VAGABOND. Oh, I'm a fairly good hand at guessing. I think I've already guessed what prompted you to leave your room and come down here to the fireside.

VIRGINIA. And what's your guess on that?

VAGABOND That you expected—or rather hoped —I'd be here.

VIRGINIA. *(Half amused, half indignant)* What!

VAGABOND. Come, let's not pretend; play the game straight-away; be truthful. I do attract you, now, don't I?

VIRGINIA. *(Serious)* You're not serious, I hope?

VAGABOND. Well, as serious as it is possible for a man to be when once he has come to realize that there is nothing altogether serious in this huge joke of life.

VIRGINIA. I never met a man like you.

VAGABOND. No. There never was a man like me.

VIRGINIA. I can almost believe that.

VAGABOND. Ah! Then I'm getting on. *(Moves his chair closer to her)* A fair question, if you don't mind?

VIRGINIA. Well?

VAGABOND. What is there about me that you admire so much?

VIRGINIA. The thing I admire most in you—is your complete admiration for yourself.

VAGABOND. Ah! A cruel thrust.

VIRGINIA. Are you cut?

VAGABOND. I'm bleeding.

VIRGINIA. Shall I heal the wound?
VAGABOND. Do.—Do, please.
VIRGINIA. I think you're very nice.
VAGABOND. *(Rises and raising his voice as he says this)* Aha, I was sure of that.
VIRGINIA. Sh-h, you'll have them down.
VAGABOND. Let them come! Let them come!— *(Puts his chair R. of table L.C. and goes to R.C.)* —and we'll both tell them—we'll tell them the truth —we'll tell them that you've changed your mind.
VIRGINIA. *(Rises)* About what?
VAGABOND. Your engagement.
VIRGINIA. Don't be silly.
VAGABOND. But surely you wouldn't marry a man you don't love?
VIRGINIA. Who said I didn't love him?
VAGABOND. You did.
VIRGINIA. When?
VAGABOND. Just now. You told me you thought me very nice.
VIRGINIA. What of that?
VAGABOND. Could a girl in love with one man so express herself to another?
VIRGINIA. *(Amused)* You're funny. I meant what I'd already told you—that you amused me.
VAGABOND. *(Meditates, faces VIRGINIA)* All right, I amuse you. *(Pauses—points, then looks upstairs)* Could *he* do as much?
VIRGINIA. Who?
VAGABOND. The man upstairs—the *villain*.
VIRGINIA. Why do you call him a villain?
VAGABOND. He may be a villain. If he's ever robbed a house, ruined a girl, or forged a name, he's a villain; a villain of the deepest dye. He might have committed a thousand crimes, who knows? Let's look him up and find out. Anyhow, there must be a villain. Oh, there's got to be a villain—so why not he?

VIRGINIA. *(Laughing)* Why, Tom Allen comes from one of the oldest families in the state.

VAGABOND. Good! Splendid! We'll trace the name back till we come to a crime—and claim we fear heredity.

VIRGINIA. What are you saying?

VAGABOND. *(Goes L., then comes back to her)* Oh, ho! I'll get you out of this. Come, my lass, never fear, I'll get you out of this! Somewhere, somehow I'll get you out of this.

VIRGINIA. Get me out of what?

VAGABOND. Your foolish promise to marry.

VIRGINIA. *(Goes to him)* But I have no desire to break my promise.

VAGABOND. You mean he is not being forced on you—that you will marry him of your own free will?

VIRGINIA. Of course.

VAGABOND. Oh, well, then it's my mistake and I ask your forgivness, and I apologize most abjectly. *(Moves L. a bit.)*

VIRGINIA. *(Over to him)* Tell me, what made you imagine that the choice was not my own?

VAGABOND. Your parents seemed so satisfied.

VIRGINIA. *(Laughs)* Oh, that's clever, terribly clever.

VAGABOND. Ah, you laugh! You laugh! 'Tis a true sign of forgiveness, I trust.

VIRGINIA. *(Crossing and extending her hand)* Of course I forgive you.

VAGABOND. *(Raises her hand to his lips)* May I? (ALLEN *appears on stairs and watches the scene below.)*

VIRGINIA. You may.

VAGABOND. *(Kisses her hand)* Oh, if only my guess had been right and I'd had a chance to fight and release you from an undesirable match. (AL-LEN *comes to landing of stairs.)* How I should have loved the drama of the thing! But, alas, the drama disappears. *(He drops her hand, dejected)* 'Tis a comic situation. *(He moves a step to* L.*)*

VIRGINIA. Which I've enjoyed immensely.

VAGABOND. Yes?

VIRGINIA. If I sleep tonight, I'll laugh in my dreams.

VAGABOND. If I sleep tonight, I'll dream of your laugh.

VIRGINIA. Goodnight.

VAGABOND. You're going?

VIRGINIA. I must. *(As the* VAGABOND *takes her hand and looks at her questioningly.)* You may. *(The* VAGABOND *kisses her hand.)*

ALLEN. *(Sternly, from stairs)* Virginia! *(*VIRGINIA *and* VAGABOND *stand glued to the spot, then* VIRGINIA *moves over* R.*)*

VAGABOND. *(To the audience)* Ah, ha, the damned thing may not be a farce, after all. *(Goes to* L. *of table* L.C.*)*

ALLEN. *(Comes quickly down* L.*, stares haughtily at* VAGABOND, *then turns to* VIRGINIA*)* Virginia, I demand an explanation. *(Crosses to* VIRGINIA.*)*

VIRGINIA. You're entitled to it, Tom. It was the log fire that attracted me. I couldn't resist the temptation. I tiptoed down the stairs when I thought the house asleep, but it seemed that this gentleman was secluded in some corner of the room, for he suddenly appeared on the scene. *(Moves over to* ALLEN*)* He's been wonderfully amusing and entertaining. I only wish you'd been here; I'm sure you'd have enjoyed him as much as I.

ALLEN. He kissed your hand. Not once, but *twice*, I saw him kiss your hand.

VAGABOND. Ah, but not without permission.

ALLEN. Speak when you're spoken to—not until then. I'll be ready for *you* in just a moment.

(VAGABOND *moves quickly down below table* L.C., *looking straight in front of him.*)

VIRGINIA. Tom, are you going mad!

ALLEN. There are men in asylums for less than this.

VIRGINIA. Don't be a fool.

ALLEN. That's just what I don't intend to be—a fool for you or any other woman. Go to your room.

VIRGINIA. What!

ALLEN. *(Pointing to stairs)* Go to your room—I command you.

VIRGINIA. *(Pause)* How dare you take that tone with me?

VAGABOND. Bravo, my lass. I applaud your grit. *(CRASH.)* Ah, ha! even the elements enter into the spirit of the scene.

MRS. LAMSON. *(Enters on stairs, calling)* Virginia! Virginia! (ALLEN *goes up to door* C.)

VIRGINIA. Yes, Mother. *(Standing at the head of the stairs,* MRS. LAMSON *looks down at* VIRGINIA *and the* TWO MEN. *After another wearied look at* VIRGINIA, *she comes down* R.C.*)*

MRS. LAMSON. *(To* VIRGINIA*)* What's happened? Is something wrong?

VIRGINIA. No, dear, it's nothing.

MRS. LAMSON. *(Looks at* VAGABOND, *who bows. She then turns to* VIRGINIA*)* Then why did you leave your room? *(Terrified, she goes quickly up to* ALLEN*)* What is it, Tom? Tell me.

ALLEN. *(Looking directly at the* VAGABOND*)* It's all right, Mrs. Lamson; everything's all right. *(Crosses* R. *to fireplace.)*

MRS. LAMSON. *(After a look at the* VAGABOND, *she goes to* VIRGINIA*)* Come, Virginia. You must get some sleep. *(She takes* VIRGINIA *to the stairs.)*

VIRGINIA. *(As she reaches the second step, she turns and looks coldly at* ALLEN, *then smiles at the* VAGABOND*)* Goodnight.

VAGABOND. *(Goes to foot of stairs, looking defiantly at* ALLEN*)* Goodnight, Miss Virginia. If you laugh in your dreams, may your dreams come true. May you laugh forever and ever.

MRS. LAMSON. Come, dear. (VIRGINIA *looks at* ALLEN, *then joins her mother and they start to exit.*) You shouldn't have left your room.

VAGABOND. *(To* ALLEN, *as he comes down* L.C.*)* Well, shall we start the scene? *(Slight pause)* Come, what's it to be, a battle of words or a smashing good fight? Take your choice, my aristocratic friend. I'm an expert at either game. (BOTH *advance and meet* C.*)*

ALLEN. I want to apologize to you, young man. *(Looking toward stairs)* I appreciate your position, your embarrassment, and I want you to know that I hold you entirely blameless. The girl's at fault. She's a bit of a flirt. I'm trying to break her of the habit, so you see it was almost necessary that I take the stand I did just now. I don't want you to think me a cad—I'm not—I'm a gentleman.

VAGABOND. A-ah!

ALLEN. And if you're one, you'll accept my apology.

VAGABOND. *(Tragic)* And is this all there is to be to the *big moment?* I'd hoped it would lead up to a strong dramatic climax. Ye gods, is there no drama left in the world? Am I to meet with this sort of disappointment the balance of my life? *(Looking front.)*

ALLEN. I've made myself clear? You understand, I hope?

VAGABOND. I understand that I'm damnably disappointed. However, I accept your apology and at the same time offer mine. I was in hopes you were a villain.

ALLEN. Villain? Ha, ha! No villain.

VAGABOND. No? No villain! Ha, ha! No drama—ha, ha! *(Comes to front of table* L.C.*)*

SALLY. *(Enters on stairs and comes to landing, calling)* Master! Master Freeman! Master Freeman!

ALLEN. What's the row, my girl?

SALLY. Where's the Master? Where's the Master?

VAGABOND. What's up?

SALLY. *(Comes down to* R. *of the* VAGABOND*)* The sick woman—she's up and dressed—ready to go. He told me to warn him if she made a move. Where's the Master?

VAGABOND. In his bed, no doubt, where Masters spend most of the time.

SALLY. I must warn him at once. *(As she starts for the stairs she sees* VIOLET *entering)* She's coming.

(VIOLET *enters at head of stairs; comes down to the landing; looks at* SALLY *and the* VAGABOND. ALLEN *stands staring at her, then turns front, a look of horror on his face.* VIOLET *comes down the stairs to* R. *as* ALLEN *turns front.)*

SALLY. *(Blocking* VIOLET'S *way)* No! You shan't go till the Master says the word.

VIOLET. *(With cold determination, not looking at* SALLY*)* Out of my way, child, before I strike you down!

SALLY. *(Cringes in fear, then rushes upstairs, calling excitedly)* Master! Master Freeman! Master Freeman! *(Exits at head of stairs.)*

VIOLET. *(With her eyes glued on* ALLEN, *she moves down* R. *They stand staring at each other)* You here!

ALLEN. *(Puzzled)* Who are you?

VIOLET. You know very well who I am, you black-hearted wretch.

VAGABOND. *(Seating himself on table. Looking front)* Ah, ha! It was worth being born to be thrilled like this.

VIOLET. What are *you* doing here?

ALLEN. *(Crosses to VIOLET)* Is this a trick, a trap? Are you trying to ruin me?

VIOLET. *You* ruined *me!*

ALLEN. Don't say that again or—*(Goes to her with raised fist)*—or I'll forget that you're a woman.

VIOLET. You can't frighten me. I'll have my revenge if I have to hound you to the end of your days.

VAGABOND. By gad, I never heard the line read better. (VIOLET *looks at him.*) Beautifully rendered, dramatically correct. Go on, my lass, let's hear some more. (VIOLET *moves over to fireplace.*)

ALLEN. *(Crosses to VAGABOND, who is still sitting on the table.* VIOLET *crosses* L.*)* Are you her accomplice? *(A pause)* What is this, some blackmailing scheme you have in mind? If it be, I warn you that you are dealing with a desperate man.

VAGABOND. Repeat those words again.

ALLEN. You're dealing with a desperate man.

VAGABOND. *(Jumps from table and goes* L., AL-LEN *backing away from him to* C.*)* Nothing like it, my boy. Do you expect me to rise to the situation when words are uttered in such a cold, colorless, mechanical way? Impossible. (ALLEN *stares at him in amazement.*) Come, put more fire, more vigor, more strength behind it all so that I may meet and combat the attack. Now, then, once more the "desperate man" line. *(Crosses extreme* L.*)*

ALLEN. *(Slight pause)* Are you trying to poke fun at me? *(Crosses to* VAGABOND, *his fist raised)* If you are, by God, I'll——

VAGABOND. *(Delighted)* That's it! Splendid.

splendid! Now for my reply. *(Crosses to* ALLEN, *who backs away)* Take care, you kid-glove ruffian, or I'll thrash you within an inch of your life. *(Draws out word "inch"—in-nin-nin-nin-ninch. Taps* ALLEN *on the chest; moves* L.) See—that means something. Now go on with the play.

ALLEN. *(To* VIOLET*)* What clown is this? Who are you two people?

VIOLET. *(Turns on* ALLEN, *laughing scornfully)* Had I known you were beneath the roof of this tavern I'd have fought my way through a million storms rather than breathe the air of the place. I hate, loathe, and despise you. I'm going to make you pay. I'm going to make you suffer. I'm going to drag you down, degrade, and destroy you. There's nothing you can do or say that will block my purpose. There's nothing I want but revenge. If, on your bended knees, you begged, implored and pleaded for mercy, I'd spit in your face and laugh with glee. *(Pause, her hand to her head)* I'm on my way to the Capitol.

ALLEN. *(Stands rigid)* To the Capitol?

VIOLET. *(Satisfied at the effect of her words, she smiles, moves over to* TOM *and says tauntingly)* That makes you think, does it not, Mr. Devil?

(GOVERNOR *enters on stairs, comes to landing and watches scene in the room below.)*

ALLEN. *(After a pause)* On your way to the Capitol!

VIOLET. *(Defiantly)* To tell my story to the Governor.

GOVERNOR. *(On landing)* To tell *what* story to the Governor? (ALL *turn and look at the* GOVERNOR.)

VAGABOND. *(Jumps up, tremendously excited)* By gad, what a smashing situation! *(Sits again on table, puts his feet on a nearby chair and watches the scene with great interest.)*

GOVERNOR. *(Comes down to* ALLEN, *who is now* R.C.*)* What did the woman mean, Tom? Who is she?

ALLEN. I don't know what she meant, Governor. I don't know who she is. *(He looks suspiciously at* VAGABOND, *then turns to the* GOVERNOR *again)* I never saw the woman before in all my life. *(Looks at* VIOLET, *makes a quick move toward the* VAGABOND, *then goes upstage* C.*)*

GOVERNOR. *(To* VIOLET, *after a searching look at the* VAGABOND*)* Did you say you were on your way to the Capitol to see Governor Lamson?

VIOLET. I did.

GOVERNOR. *(Crossing to* VIOLET*)* I am Governor Lamson.

VIOLET. *You!*

GOVERNOR. I am. (FREEMAN *enters on stairs and watches the scene below.* VIOLET *tries to speak, but her throat goes dry. Her strength gives way under the strain, she closes her eyes, sways, loses her balance and falls in* GOVERNOR'S *arms in a dead faint.)* The woman's fainted.

VAGABOND. *(To the audience)* Damn the luck! 'Twould have been a great scene but for that. *(During the above lines* ALLEN *has gradually worked his way upstage to door* C.*)*

ALLEN. *(Swings the door open and dashes out into storm, uttering a cry of fear)* God! *(CRASH.)*

VAGABOND. *(Jumps from table as he sees* ALLEN *rushing out)* He's gone! *(Quickly closes and bars door and dances down above table* L.C.*)* He's gone! He's gone!

(SALLY *runs on from stairs, screaming in terror.)*

FREEMAN. Quiet, Sally. (MRS. LAMSON *and*

VIRGINIA *appear at head of stairs and join* SALLY.)
  VAGABOND. *(Exulting)* He's gone!
  FREEMAN. *(Goes to* GOVERNOR*)* I'll take her, Your Excellency. (FREEMAN *takes* VIOLET *from* GOVERNOR. MRS. LAMSON *and* VIRGINIA *come down the stairs.)*
  VAGABOND. *(Back of table,* L.C.*)* He's gone!
  GOVERNOR. *(Goes upstage and peers out through window)* Why in Heaven's name should he dash out into the storm?
  VIRGINIA. *(Coming down* R.*)* What is it, Dad?
  MRS. LAMSON. *(Following* VIRGINIA *down* R.*)* What is it? What's happened? (FREEMAN *carries* VIOLET *to first landing.)*
  VAGABOND. *(To* VIRGINIA*)* He's gone, my lass. You're free, free as the air; rid of the man you would have married of your own free will. Ha! ha! He's gone! (*The* GOVERNOR, MRS. LAMSON *and* VIRGINIA *go to* L. *window and look out.)* Ah, ha! He's gone! He's gone! *(Goes to* FREEMAN, *who is still holding* VIOLET*)* Proceed, Mr. Landlord. (FREEMAN *exits upstairs.)* Once more I see the betrayed, deserted maiden carried to her downy couch where she may sleep and dream her dreams of vengeance sweet. *(Going up to stairs)* Ah, what a night! What a delightfully dramatic night! And how fortunate that I should have happened here on a night like this. There had to be a hero. 'Twould have been a dull, old tavern without a hero tonight. (FREEMAN *comes down to landing.)* *(CRASH.)* *(The* VAGABOND *is now on landing)* What a storm! What a storm! How I envy the man who is out in a storm like this. Clever dog, that villain, to have even thought of the idea. What a night! What a glorious storm! *(Exit upstairs.)*   *(CRASH.)*

(FREEMAN *crosses and peers out through window.*

Virginia *and* Mrs. Lamson *come down above armchair* R.)

Mrs. Lamson. What does it all mean, Robert?

Governor. I'm as much at sea as you, my dear.

Freeman. *(Peering out of window)* Without coat or hat in a storm like this! Good Lord, the man will die. *(Comes down below table* L.C.*)*

Mrs. Lamson. *(To* Virginia*)* What was he saying a while ago when I found him with you in this room?

Governor. In this room—tonight!

Mrs. Lamson. Yes, but not alone. This other man was with them.

Governor. What? Virginia!

Virginia. He found me with the other man and took a tone I did not like. I told him so—and we had words.

Governor. Who is this other man?

Virginia. He would not say. I wish I knew—for he's the quaintest man I ever met. (Mrs. Lamson *looks apprehensively at her husband, crying "Virginia."*)

Governor. *(Looks upstairs, then comes down* L.C. *to* Freeman*)* Who is he, landlord; his name?

Freeman. That he refuses to give. Who he is and from whence he comes is a mystery to us all. He and this woman were discovered. 'Twas my own son who gave the alarm.

Governor. When was that?

Freeman. This very night, less than an hour before you arrived.

Virginia. *(Going to* R.C.*)* You say he travels in company with this woman?

Freeman. He denies the fact and vows they never met before tonight, but I fear he lies. They're conspirators, I swear.

Virginia. I don't believe it.

Mrs. Lamson. Virginia!

Virginia. I don't, Mother. I don't believe that man would lie.

Governor. *(A slight pause, then he goes to Virginia)* What do *you* know of the man?

Virginia. Nothing—but I'd believe anything he'd say.

Governor *and* Mrs. Lamson. *(Indignant)* Virginia!

Governor. What possible connection could Tom Allen have with such a pair?

Virginia. I don't know. It's baffling, Dad. (All *cross to window.*) *(CRASH.)*

Governor. He'll perish on a night like this. *(Comes down above table* l.c.*)*

Freeman. He's mad to try to fight such a storm, Your Excellency.

Governor. *(Crosses to* Freeman*)* The woman claims she was on her way to the Capitol.

Freeman. To see you, yes. She told us that before you came.

Mrs. Lamson. *(Crossing to* Governor*)* What could she want, Robert?

Governor. I can't imagine, dear. It's all very mystifying, very strange.

Vagabond. *(Enters on stairs and comes down to first step)* Hush! (All *turn to him.*) All is well with the fainting female. She sleeps most peacefully and snores delightfully. *(Waving in the direction of the sleeping rooms)* Sleep on, fair maiden of the woodshed. May your troubles disappear in slumberland as they would in death. *(Comes to* c.*)* That is possible, my friends, that is quite possible, for who was it said that "death is but an awakening to find that life itself is but a dream." *(Sings and dances)*

As big as a cow, but as tame as a calf,
She settles the problems of life with a laugh.

(He looks at MRS. LAMSON, *who goes around him to* R. *He turns to* VIRGINIA *with a smile. Interspersed with song—dances a bit)* A dancing relief, so to speak. But what about the *villain?* Has he returned, or am I to be made happy with the thought that he is shivering and shaking on the lonely road in the dead of night, as our comic friend, the landlord, so gruesomely paints the picture?

GOVERNOR. *(Goes* C. *to* VAGABOND*)* You must answer a few questions, young man.

VAGABOND. Question me to your heart's content, Your Excellency. You'll find my answer quick, direct and to the point.

GOVERNOR. *(Going to* MRS. LAMSON*)* Mother—(VAGABOND *moves down to* R. *of table* L.C., *giving* FREEMAN *a look.* FREEMAN *turns away.)*

MRS. LAMSON. Yes, Robert?

GOVERNOR. You and Virginia go to your rooms. *(Takes her up to foot of stairs.)*

MRS. LAMSON. *(As they go upstage)* Yes, dear, but I'll not sleep a wink knowing that Tom is out there in the storm.

GOVERNOR. There's a reason for it all—we'll soon know. *(Turns to his daughter)* Virginia.

VIRGINIA. Yes, Dad.

GOVERNOR. Go with your mother. (VAGABOND *crosses to* VIRGINIA *at stairs.)*

MRS. LAMSON. Come, dear. *(Going upstairs.)*

VIRGINIA. *(To* VAGABOND*)* Who is the woman upstairs?

GOVERNOR. *(Sternly)* Don't question the man. I'll do that. *(Crosses to fireplace.)*

VIRGINIA. *(Goes upstairs, then turns to* VAGABOND*)* Good night.

VAGABOND. *(Moving up to newel post)* Good night, most charming daughter of an illustrious father. I don't know who she is or why she is, but if you ask me what she is, I'll say a stranger so far as I'm concerned.

MRS. LAMSON. *(Impatiently)* Come, Virginia. (VIRGINIA *goes to landing on stairs and again turns to* VAGABOND.)

VAGABOND. *(Bowing to* MRS. LAMSON*)* Good night, most helpful mother of the charming daughter of an illustrious father. May your dreams be as radiant and rare as the sweet and gracious child at your side. *(Bows to each in turn as he mentions them.)*

MRS. LAMSON. *(To* VIRGINIA, *after a slight pause)* Come, dear. *(She and* VIRGINIA *start up the stairs, turn and look at the* VAGABOND, *who again bows; then the* WOMEN *exit.)*

FREEMAN. (L. *of table* L.C.*)* Shall I go or stay, Excellency?

GOVERNOR. *(*R.*)* Stay where you are, landlord.

VAGABOND. *(Coming down* C.*)* Oh, by all means, friend Freeman, stay and witness an exhibition of criss-cross questioning and rapid-fire answering that might well be worth the hearing. I stand ready to be probed, Your Most Magnificent Excellency. *(Makes the* GOVERNOR *a sweeping bow.)*

GOVERNOR. *(Crossing to* VAGABOND, *out of patience)* This is no time for levity. Who are you?

VAGABOND. Question number one: The inevitable "Who are you?" The answer is, I don't know who I am and if I did I'd be the most miserable man on earth, for my greatest happiness lies in the fact that I occupy a most unique position—that of not having been cast for a part in the great world drama of life. *(Slight pause)* I am a lonely, single-handed spectator sitting back looking on and laughing at the monkey-shines of the great all-star company of several billions of men and women who are unknowingly playing the piece for me—they're playing the piece for me. I am the audience, but a good audience, withal, for I laugh—— I am the audience, and if I may say so, a highly intellectual audience, for in all the changing scenes of this ever-beginning, never-ending plotless plot, I recognize the spiritual hand of a great director, a master director, who has so skillfully staged this tightly woven, disconnected, tightly knitted spectacle of tragic nonsense, and so I am amused, and I laugh, and I applaud. (VAGABOND *applauds*) And if I'm any critic, it's a bully good show, and I hope some day to meet the author, and compliment him upon his marvelous entertainment. Alas, I have no one with whom I may discuss the merits of the play, for all the rest are on the stage. I'm sitting out in front, alone, all alone. *(Backs up stage a few paces; turns to* GOVERNOR, *whom he addresses)* Do you follow me, Your Excellency?

GOVERNOR. Sounds like the ravings of a madman. I don't understand you at all.

VAGABOND. Of course you don't. I'd have been horribly disappointed if you had.

GOVERNOR. Disappointed?

VAGABOND. *(Crosses to* GOVERNOR*)* Yes, disappointed that a man brilliant enough to have understood me should waste his time on an ordinary political career.

GOVERNOR. Enough of this nonsense! Who is this companion of yours, this female upstairs?

VAGABOND. She's no companion of mine, Your Excellency! 'Tis but a woodshed acquaintance.

GOVERNOR. A woodshed acquaintance?

VAGABOND. Yes, Your Excellency. Have you never met a girl in a woodshed?

GOVERNOR. How dare you—how dare you suggest such a thing?

VAGABOND. Ah! 'Tis not a suggestion. You misapprehend.

FREEMAN. Do you realize that you're speaking to the Governor?

VAGABOND. Yes, I have a very full realization of the fact, but for some unknown reason you seem to imagine that you're part of the conversation.

GOVERNOR. *(Crosses to* VAGABOND*)* What did this woman do to cast a spell over my friend and frighten him away? What did she say?

VAGABOND. That she was on her way to the Capitol for a personal interview with you.

GOVERNOR. And why should that information drive him out into the night?

VAGABOND. I didn't write the play, Your Excellency. As I explained to you a few moments ago, I'm sitting out in front looking on.

GOVERNOR. *(Testily)* You talk in circles.

VAGABOND. It's square talk, nevertheless.

GOVERNOR. *(Pause)* What's your game?

VAGABOND. Chess, cards or dominoes. I'm expert at all three.

GOVERNOR. *(Nearer to the* VAGABOND*)* Why don't you answer my questions?

VAGABOND. Why do you question my answers?

GOVERNOR. What brought you here tonight?

VAGABOND. *(Slight pause)* Fate, perhaps— *(CRASH)*—though the elements also seem to have conspired in my behalf and lured me into what begins to look like a chain of rather interesting events. *(He moves up* R.*)*

GOVERNOR. *(Looks suspiciously at* VAGABOND. *Goes to* FREEMAN, *who is below table* L.C.*)* Landlord, I believe this man to be a member of the band that held up my coach an hour ago.

FREEMAN. That may be so, Your Excellency.

VAGABOND. *(Coming down* C.*)* Ah, ha! *(To the* GOVERNOR*)* I was sure you thought that, but my alibi is complete. I was here an hour ago—two hours ago. *(To* FREEMAN*)* You know that. Why do you lie and try to implicate me?

FREEMAN. *(Going to* VAGABOND, *the* GOVERNOR *below table* L.C.*)* Because you refuse to say who you are, from where you hail, for where you are bound, or why you are here. You're a suspicious character—so is the woman. *(To the* GOVERNOR, *the* VAGABOND *going to the fireplace)* I suggest they both be placed under arrest, Your Excellency. (VAGABOND *gets fire irons.*)

GOVERNOR. For political reasons I did not intend the hold-up should be made public, but we must get to the bottom of this. I'll take your advice. Send for the police, landlord.

FREEMAN. I've already done that.

VAGABOND. *What?*

FREEMAN. *(To* GOVERNOR*)* I took the liberty, Your Excellency, and dispatched my man for the Sheriff an hour ago.

(ZACH *knocks on door* C.*)*

VAGABOND. They'll have to win a fight before they take me.

FREEMAN. *(Goes up* C. *Barring* VAGABOND'S *way)* Who's there?

ZACH. *(Off* C.*)* 'Tis I, Father—Zach. Open the door. (FREEMAN *unbars and throws open door.*)
(CRASH.)

(VAGABOND *returns fire irons.* ZACH *enters, followed by* WILLUM. VAGABOND *sits on a stool near fire.* ZACH *extinguishes the light in lantern and places it in the corner* R. *of the door.* FREEMAN *closes door and bars it and comes down* R. *of table* L.C.*)*

FREEMAN. *(To* ZACH*)* Well?

ACT II THE TAVERN 73

ZACH. *(Going to R. of his father)* Willum says the Sheriff was not at home.

FREEMAN. The Sheriff not at home!

WILLUM. *(R.)* Hasn't been home all night; that's what his wife said.

FREEMAN. You saw his wife?

WILLUM. Yes, and now that I've seen her I wouldn't be surprised if he never went home.

VAGABOND. Ah, ha, a yokel with an eye for a woman! *(Laughs delightedly)* Not such a fool as he looks. (WILLUM *leans over armchair R.; stares at* VAGABOND.)

GOVERNOR. *(To* VAGABOND*)* Be quiet! *(Facing front)* Why should the Sheriff be out on a night like this?

FREEMAN. *(Facing* GOVERNOR*)* Why should *anybody* be out on a night like this?

WILLUM. I wish to God you'd thought of that before you sent me on the trip.

ZACH. *(Crosses to* FREEMAN*)* Father, why did the young man run bareheaded from the tavern?

FREEMAN. You saw him?

ZACH. Yes, I called "Halt!" but he threw me off and ran North, fighting the storm like a demon. (GOVERNOR *crosses to window.* FREEMAN *sits at table* L.C.*)*

WILLUM. *(Looks at* VAGABOND *and the* GOVERNOR *and crosses to* FREEMAN*)* What's all the strangers a-doin' here? What's the tavern full of strangers for?

FREEMAN. Go to your room, Willum.

WILLUM. *(Starts upstage, then back to* FREEMAN*)* Who's all the strangers?

FREEMAN. *(Angrily)* Go to your room!

WILLUM. *(Going toward stairs)* It was cruel sending me on a trip like that—cruelty to animals. The horse will never forgive you for sending her on a trip like that.

FREEMAN. *(Yells)* Go to bed!

WILLUM. What kind of a night is this, anyway? What's the mystery all about? What did you want the Sheriff for? What's the strangers doin' here? (VIOLET *starts shrieking at the top of her voice.* WILLUM *rushes to* R. *side of stairs and looks up*) Who's the woman a-screamin'? What's goin' on here, anyway?

SALLY. *(Runs on at head of stairs, calling excitedly)* Master! Master Freeman!

FREEMAN. *(Up to foot of stairs)* Yes, Sally?

SALLY. The sick woman—she's up again!

FREEMAN *and* GOVERNOR. *What?*

SALLY. She tried to climb out of the window. I grabbed her just in time.

FREEMAN. Hurry, Sally, make sure she doesn't escape.

SALLY. Yes, good Master. *(Runs upstairs and off.)*

WILLUM. *(Mystified)* What is it, a joke? Somebody tryin' to play a joke on me? Who is this feller? *(Indicating* VAGABOND. VAGABOND *mocks* WILLUM, *singing and laughing.)*

FREEMAN. Quick, Zach! *(Grabs his shotgun)* Here——

ZACH. *(Rushing to* FREEMAN*)* Yes, Father.

FREEMAN. *(Giving* ZACH *the gun)* Hold the man safe. Shoot him like a dog if he starts for the door.

ZACH. Trust me for that.

FREEMAN. I'll see what the woman's up to, Your Excellency. *(Starts for the stairs.)*

GOVERNOR. *(Going up* R.*)* I'll go with you, landlord.

FREEMAN. Shoot if he moves, son.

GOVERNOR. *(To* ZACH*)* Take no chances, boy. Shoot to kill.

ZACH. I understand.

FREEMAN. *(On landing)* After you, Your Excellency.

GOVERNOR. Come, hurry. *(Exits quickly, followed by* FREEMAN.*)*

VAGABOND. *(To* ZACH*)* Lower the gun, boy; don't strain your nerves.

ZACH. *(Keeping* VAGABOND *covered)* Keep your mouth shut or I'll send you to Kingdom Come. (SHERIFF *KNOCKS on door* C. *Pause.)* Who's there?

SHERIFF. *(Off* C.*)* Open the door.

ZACH. Who would enter? *(Frightened.)*

SHERIFF. *(KNOCKS again)* Open the door in the name of the Law!

ZACH. *(Frightened, he turns to* VAGABOND*)* In the name of the Law?

VAGABOND. *(Rises)* Ah, ha! The police have arrived! Now for the melodramatics. Open the door, boy, and let's get at the thing.

SHERIFF. *(Off* C.*)* Open the door. (ZACH *unbars door and comes down* L.; *puts down gun.)*
(CRASH.)

(The VAGABOND *moves over* R. TWO COPS *enter and cover* ZACH *and the* VAGABOND *with their guns.)*

1ST COP. *(Down* R.C.*)* Hands up, everybody! (ZACH *and* VAGABOND *put up their hands.)*

2ND COP. *(Down* L.*)* Steady! Stand where you are.

1ST COP. *(Backs up to door* C. *and calls)* All right, Sheriff.

(The SHERIFF *enters.) (CRASH.)* (TONY, 3D COP, *carrying the lifeless form of* TOM ALLEN *over his shoulder, comes down* C. 2ND COP *closes and bars the door.)*

SHERIFF. *(To* COPS*)* Search these men. Make sure they're not armed. This one I'll put near the fire to thaw out. He's more frightened than hurt, I think. (TONY *drops* ALLEN *in the armchair near the fireplace, while the* TWO COPS *frisk* ZACH *and the* VAGABOND.*)* Outside, Tony. (2ND COP *opens door as* TONY *exits, then closes it.)* *(CRASH.)*

1ST COP. *(R.)* Nothing on this man.

2ND COP. *(L.)* This one neither.

SHERIFF. *(To* ALLEN, *who is still unconscious)* Well, my brave and fearless bucko, if you'd had the sense to quit running when I called to you to stop, I wouldn't have had to wing you. *(To* 1ST COP*)* Take a look at his wound, Ezra, and see if he's badly hurt. *(He comes to* C. 1ST COP *unwinds the handkerchief from* ALLEN'S *wrist and examines the wound.)*

VAGABOND. *(As he recognizes* ALLEN*)* Well, well, as I live, 'tis the villain himself—and in the clutches of the Law. Justice will be done. *(Laughs delightedly.)*

SHERIFF. What do you mean? Do you know this man?

VAGABOND. Yes. He's the intended husband of Governor Lamson's daughter.

SHERIFF. What are you saying?

ZACH. *(Below table* L.C.*)* He speaks the truth, Sheriff. That man was one of the Governor's party when they arrived tonight.

SHERIFF. The Governor arrived here tonight!

VAGABOND. Along with his most helpful wife, and extremely charming daughter. You'll find them on the landing above, if you doubt my word.

ZACH. It's true, Sheriff. They're all upstairs.

SHERIFF. Governor——! *(He looks from one to the other, backs upstage and looks toward stairs, then turns to the* 1ST COP, *who is examining* AL-

LEN's *arm)* Looks as if we'd shot our way into society, Ezra. *(Indicating* ALLEN*)* How is he?

1ST COP. He'll be all right. It's nothing but a scratch.

SHERIFF. *(After another suspicious look at* ZACH *and the* VAGABOND, *he comes down* C.*)* What's the Governor doing here?

VAGABOND. On his way to the Capitol.

ZACH. Driven in by the storm.

SHERIFF. Who are you two men?

ZACH. I'm the tavern-keeper's son.

SHERIFF. *(To* VAGABOND*)* And you?

VAGABOND. What does it matter who I am so long as I'm somebody's son?

SHERIFF. No insolence. Who are you?

ZACH. No use, Sheriff, he won't say who he is. We've been trying to find out all night.

SHERIFF. I don't follow you.

ZACH. This man and a mysterious woman turned up several hours ago, but they won't tell who they are.

SHERIFF. Where is the mysterious woman?

ZACH. Upstairs.

SHERIFF. And the Governor's upstairs, you say?

ZACH. Yes.

VAGABOND. Along with his most helpful wife and extremely charming daughter.

SHERIFF. My old woman said that someone came while I was out and told of a round-up here at the tavern.

ZACH. That was the hired man who saw your wife.

VAGABOND. Yes, and when he saw your wife he understood why you were out.

SHERIFF. *(Gives* VAGABOND *a black look, goes* L.C., *looks at him again, then moves over to* ZACH*)* Where *is* this hired man?

ZACH. Upstairs.

SHERIFF. Where's your father?

ZACH. Upstairs.

SHERIFF. Quite a gathering upstairs.

VAGABOND. Aye, a joyous and gladsome gathering, a jovial group of characters. It only needed the arrival of the Sheriff with his tin badge to make it a perfect evening of rollicking, romantic, melodramatic joy; gripping, intense, "never a dull moment," as the playbills read.

SHERIFF. *(Turns to* ZACH, *mystified by* VAGABOND'S *words)* What's the matter with this fellow?

ZACH. That's what we're all wondering.

SHERIFF. *(Indicating* ALLEN*)* And why was this other one running through the storm like a wild man?

ZACH. The whole thing's a mystery, Sheriff.

SHERIFF. *(Backing up* C.*)* I'll soon clear up the mystery. Ezra!

1ST COP. Yes?

SHERIFF. Joshua!

2ND COP. *(Over to* SHERIFF*)* Yes?

SHERIFF. Guard the tavern from the outside and spare no ammunition on any man, woman or child that attempts to escape.

BOTH COPS. Yes.

SHERIFF. *(Unbarring the* C. *door)* If I need you here, I'll signal with the shot of the gun. Understand?

BOTH COPS. Yes.

SHERIFF. Go on, men. *(Opening the door.)*
(CRASH.)

(COPS *exit.* SHERIFF *bars door after crash.*)

VAGABOND. *(As* COPS *exit)* Ah, ha, the action begins! The detective sets to work! By gad, the thing has all the elements of a hair-raising thriller.

SHERIFF. *(Coming down* C.*)* You seem to be getting a lot of fun out of this.

VAGABOND. *(Laughing)* Surely you wouldn't have me take this seriously?

ALLEN. *(Regaining consciousness but still dazed)* Where am I?

VAGABOND. *(Laughing at* ALLEN*)* Ha, ha!

ALLEN. What's happened?

VAGABOND. Ho, ho!

ALLEN. Have I been dreaming?

VAGABOND. He, he!

ALLEN. *(Noticing his wounded arm)* What's the matter with my arm?

VAGABOND. Ah, ha! The villain revives.

SHERIFF. *(To* ALLEN*)* Take it easy, young fellow. (ALLEN *looks in wonder at* SHERIFF. VIOLET *starts screaming horribly upstairs.* ZACH *and the* SHERIFF *turn quickly to the stairs.)* What's that?

ZACH. It's the mysterious woman.

VIOLET. *(Off upstairs)* All right, all right, I'll tell everything—everything there is to tell.

(SHERIFF *and* ZACH *tiptoe upstairs during the following speech, standing with their backs to audience, listening to* VIOLET. *The* VAGABOND *moves up to foot of stairs.)*

VIOLET. *(Upstairs)* I was a slip of a girl with my school-books under my arm. He was the son of a millionaire. We met. He wooed me. I fell in love. He ruined my life. (VAGABOND *comes down* R. *of the armchair, pointing his finger derisively at* ALLEN, *forcing the latter out of his chair.)* —And turned me into the streets to become what I am today. I'll pay him back! I'll hound him to his grave. (ALLEN *rises, terror-stricken, and works his way slowly up to door* C., *followed by* VAGABOND, *who grins with fiendish delight at* ALLEN's *fright.*) Vengeance shall be mine. I swear it! (ALLEN *unbars the door and again rushes out into the storm, uttering cries of fear.*) (*CRASH.*)

VAGABOND. (*He has never taken his eyes from* ALLEN) Ah, ha! He's gone again! (*Comes down* C.)

SHERIFF. (*Coming down* C.) Who?

VAGABOND. The villain.

SHERIFF. What?

(*Four pistol SHOTS are heard off, after the* SHERIFF *rushes out.*) (*CRASH.*)

(VAGABOND *dashes up, closes and bars the door; dances and sings, shouting, "He's gone! He's gone!" CRASHES of THUNDER continue until* VAGABOND *is seated on table* L.C. FREEMAN *and the* GOVERNOR *appear on the stairs.*)

FREEMAN. What's the matter, son? What's happened? (*Comes down* L.C.)

ZACH. The Sheriff's arrived.

FREEMAN. Where is he?

ZACH. He's gone.

FREEMAN. Arrived and gone? What do you mean? (*Two pistol SHOTS.*)

WILLUM. (*Appearing at the head of the stairs*) Who's doin' all the shootin'? What's all the shootin' for?

FREEMAN. Be quiet, Willum.

WILLUM. (*Coming down to* FREEMAN) What's the shootin' for?

FREEMAN. Be quiet, I say.

MRS. LAMSON. (*Appears with* VIRGINIA *at the head of the stairs*) What is it, Robert? What's wrong?

SALLY. (*Appearing at the head of the stairs*) What's happened, Zach? (*SIX SHOTS.*)

WILLUM. What's all the shootin' for?

VAGABOND. *(Speaking out front)* Sh-h! A big melodramatic moment—the ticking of the clock. *(FOUR STROKES on METRONOME.)* The dropping of a pin. *(He takes a pin from the lapel of his coat and drops it. HEAVY THUD off stage.)* 'Tis indeed a spellbinding situation. *(Turns and faces door, as KNOCK of SHERIFF is heard.)*

FREEMAN. Who would enter?

SHERIFF. *(Off stage)* Open the door in the name of the Law. *(FREEMAN motions to ZACH, who comes from stair landing, unbars and opens the door.) (CRASH.) (Two COPS enter as in previous scene.)*

1ST COP. *(Down R.)* Hands up, everybody.

2ND COP. *(Down L.)* Steady, stand where you are.

1ST COP. *(Calling to off stage)* All right, Sheriff. *(CRASH.)*

SHERIFF. *(Enters as before, accompanied by TONY, who is carrying the apparently lifeless body of ALLEN on his shoulder; comes down C. ZACH closes and bars the door)* I didn't want to have to shoot this feller again, but he just won't stop running away.

GOVERNOR. *(Coming to the R. of the SHERIFF)* Good God! It's Tom Allen.

VIRGINIA. *(Comes down R., and clings to her mother in fright)* Mother!

MRS. LAMSON. Be calm, dear.

FREEMAN. *(Stepping forward)* Hello, Sheriff!

SHERIFF. Hello, Freeman. Show me to a room. I want to lock him in so he can't get away again.

FREEMAN. *(Advancing up stairs)* Right this way, Sheriff.

GOVERNOR. Just a moment, Sheriff. I am Governor Lamson.

SHERIFF. *(Almost ignoring the* GOVERNOR. *As he passes)* Glad to meet you, Governor. *(Goes to the third landing, turns and addresses the* COPS*)* Stand guard outside, boys. Keep close watch, and shoot 'em down as fast as they go through the door, understand?

ALL COPS. Right, Sheriff.

*(*ZACH *unbars and opens door.) (CRASH.) (*1ST *and* 2ND COPS *exit.* ZACH *closes and bars door as soon as they are off.)*

FREEMAN. *(On landing)* Right this way, Sheriff. *(Exits, followed by* TONY *carrying* ALLEN. SALLY *follows the* SHERIFF *off.)*

WILLUM. *(To* GOVERNOR, *indicating* ALLEN*)* What's the matter with him? *(The* GOVERNOR *makes no reply.)* What the hell kind of a night is this, anyway? *(Backing up stairs)* What kind of a night is this, anyway? *(He exits, followed by* ZACH.*)*

GOVERNOR. *(To* VAGABOND*)* It's about time we found out who you are. There's no chance to escape till you disclose your identity. Perhaps you'll sing a different tune then.

VAGABOND. (L. *of table* L.C.*)* No, the same tune —my favorite song. *(Sings and dances)*

　As big as a cow, but as tame as a calf,
　She settles the problems of life with a laugh.

(Turns to GOVERNOR*)* Pretty?

MRS. LAMSON. *(Comes down to* GOVERNOR*)* Robert——

GOVERNOR. Yes, dear?

MRS. LAMSON. That Sheriff——

GOVERNOR. The Sheriff?

MRS. LAMSON. Did you recognize his voice?

GOVERNOR. What do you mean?

Mrs. Lamson. He's one of the men who held up our coach. I'll swear it.

Governor. You're mistaken, dear.

Virginia. She's right, Dad. I saw his face as he dropped his mask and jumped on his horse to ride away.

Governor. Are you sure?

Virginia. I'm certain.

Mrs. Lamson. So am I.

Vagabond. I claim an apology, Governor. You accused me a while ago.

Sheriff. *(Off, upstairs)* All right, Freeman. I'll put him under arrest right away. (All *turn and look toward stairs.*)

Virginia. *(Moving to* R.C.*)* Put who under arrest? (Mrs. Lamson *crosses to fireplace.*)

Governor. *(To* Virginia*)* Sh-h!

Sheriff. *(Enters and comes down to* R. *of* Governor. *Referring to* Vagabond*)* Governor, the landlord tells me that you suspect this man of holding up your coach as you turned off the Pike from the Burtonville road. Is that true?

Governor. *(After high-sign from* Vagabond*)* Yes, I think he's the man, Sheriff.

Sheriff. I'll search him and see. *(Crosses to* Vagabond, *whipping out his gun)* Up with your hands! *(The* Vagabond *obeys.*)

Governor. *(Extending his hand for the* Sheriff's *gun)* Sheriff, I'll keep him covered while you see what he's got.

Sheriff. *(Slightly suspicious, he hands* Governor *gun)* If you please. *(Starts to frisk* Vagabond.*)*

Governor. *(Aiming gun at* Sheriff*)* Come on, Sheriff. Put 'em up!

Sheriff. Eh?

Governor. Put 'em up!

SHERIFF. *(Swings around to find himself covered)* What are you getting at?

VAGABOND. *(Taking in the situation)* Shall I oblige, Governor?

GOVERNOR. If you will.

VAGABOND. *(Swings* SHERIFF *around and starts going through his pockets)* And now to relieve the swaggering Sheriff of the swag.

SHERIFF. *(Menacingly)* Wait a minute. Don't forget that you're dealing with the Law.

VAGABOND. *(Gaily)* Ah, but I'm going to break the Law—break you good—take all you've got.

SHERIFF. You'll pay for this.

(FREEMAN *enters at head of stairs and stands watching the scene below, petrified with astonishment.)*

VAGABOND. No more than you paid for this. *(Finds a bracelet in* SHERIFF'S *pocket)* A jeweled bracelet!

VIRGINIA. That's mine.

VAGABOND. *(Throws a bracelet to the* GOVERNOR, *who passes it over to* VIRGINIA. *The* VAGABOND *continues his search and finds a necklace in another pocket)* A string of pearls!

MRS. LAMSON. That's mine. (VAGABOND *throws the pearls to the* GOVERNOR, *who passes the string over to his wife.)*

VAGABOND. *(Finds bag of gold on the* SHERIFF) A bag of gold!

GOVERNOR. That's mine. (VAGABOND *throws bag to the* GOVERNOR.)

VAGABOND. *(Finds a bottle of rum)* A flask of rum! Ha, ha! *(Kisses the bottle)* That's mine!

SHERIFF. What?

FREEMAN. *(Coming down,* R.C.) What does this **mean**, Your Excellency?

ACT II   THE TAVERN   85

GOVERNOR. *(Still keeping the* SHERIFF *covered)* It means, landlord, that at last we have discovered the notorious terror of the Burtonville road.

FREEMAN. What? *(The* SHERIFF *turns to the* GOVERNOR.*)*

GOVERNOR. The highway robber about whom the opposition party has so severely criticized my whole administration. *(To* VAGABOND*)* Can you find anything more, young man?

VAGABOND. Only these. *(Holds up handcuffs)* I think they belong to him.

GOVERNOR. I'm sure they do. Let's see how he looks with them on.

VAGABOND. Come on, Sheriff, the family jewelry awaits. (VAGABOND *handcuffs* SHERIFF.)

SHERIFF. *(Subdued)* All right, you've got me.

VAGABOND. Yes, and we intend to keep you.

GOVERNOR. Landlord——

FREEMAN. Yes, Your Excellency?

GOVERNOR. Lead this man to a room without a window. We'll keep him safe under lock and key until we're ready to go.

FREEMAN. *(Starting for stairs)* I will indeed, Your Excellency.

GOVERNOR. Follow the landlord, Mr. Sheriff, and keep looking straight ahead.

SHERIFF. *(Utterly cowed)* I'm not thinking of myself. I'm thinking of the wife and the twelve children.

GOVERNOR. *(To* VAGABOND*)* He's thinking of his wife!

VAGABOND. Twelve children. Ye gods, did he *ever* think of his wife?

(The SHERIFF *starts for stairs.* ZACH *has entered and is now on landing.* WILLUM *has followed* ZACH *on and stands on* L. *end of landing.)*

FREEMAN. Zach, find the key to the coatroom door; it's the only one without a window.

ZACH. What's happened, Father?

FREEMAN. What more could happen? The Sheriff's a thief, a highway robber.

ZACH. What?

FREEMAN. Find the key to the coatroom. Be quick.

ZACH. Yes, Father. *(He hurries upstairs and off.)*

FREEMAN. *(Takes gun. To SHERIFF)* This way, Sheriff. Follow that boy. I'll feel safer behind you. *(He follows the SHERIFF upstairs and off.)*

WILLUM. *(Coming down R.C.)* What's the matter now? What's goin' on now? Who the hell ever heard of a Sheriff bein' handcuffed? What's the handcuffs for? For the love of God, will somebody tell me what's happening in the tavern tonight? *(Goes to L.C.)*

GOVERNOR. *(Crossing to VIRGINIA)* Virginia, you and your mother go to your rooms.

VIRGINIA. *(Starting for stairs)* Yes, Dad. Come, Mother.

MRS. LAMSON. *(Going to GOVERNOR)* What are you going to do, Robert?

GOVERNOR. I don't know. I must think. Go to your rooms.

VAGABOND. I'd advise that, ladies. (MRS. LAMSON *goes to R. of staircase.)*

WILLUM. *(Over to GOVERNOR)* Why did they handcuff the Sheriff? What's the handcuffs for?

GOVERNOR. *(Going up R.)* Be quiet, you fool!

WILLUM. *(Over to VAGABOND)* What's the matter with all you people? What kind of a night is this, anyway?

VAGABOND. A wonderful night! The night of nights! The most glorious night of my life! *(Sings and dances around WILLUM)*

As big as a cow, but as tame as a calf,
She settles the problems of life with a laugh.

WILLUM. *(To* GOVERNOR, *pointing to* VAGABOND*)* What's the matter with *him?* (VIOLET *is heard SCREAMING off upstairs. The* VAGABOND *goes to* L. *of table* L.C. GOVERNOR R. WILLUM *above table* L.C. MRS. LAMSON *and* VIRGINIA *retreat few paces.)*

VIOLET. *(Backs on downstairs, crying hysterically)* Why is he under arrest? Why are they taking him away? What has he done? Why is he handcuffed? *(To* VIRGINIA, *who is* L. *of stairs)* Tell me, I must know. Tell me, why is he under arrest?

VIRGINIA. It's all right; be calm.

VIOLET. Be calm! How can I be calm when they're taking me from the only man I ever cared for, the only man I ever loved. They're taking him away! *Why* are they taking him away?

GOVERNOR. You mean the Sheriff?

VIOLET. Yes, yes. How can they be so cruel? *(Looking upstairs.)*

WILLUM. *(To* VAGABOND*)* What's the matter with *her?* *(Comes down* R.*)*

VIOLET. *(Coming down* R.C.*)* Haven't I suffered enough without this? Why must they add to my agony by taking from me the one man who has stood by me through all my terrible grief and struggles?

GOVERNOR. *(Coming down* C.*)* The Sheriff is your friend, you say?

VIOLET. Yes, yes, my one friend; my only friend. Why are they taking him away?

GOVERNOR. Because the man is a scoundrel who has converted the Sheriff's high office into a clearing-house for stolen goods.

VIOLET. *(Shrieks.* WILLUM, *frightened, works around to* R.*)* It's a lie; it's a lie; a terrible lie! He's a fine man, a good man, a true man, an honest man.

(Going to GOVERNOR*)* Save him, save him! Have pity, have mercy, for the sake of our child—— *(Falls at* GOVERNOR's *feet)* —the little child. Save him for the sake of the child!

GOVERNOR. For the sake of the *child!*

VAGABOND. Ah, ha! Thirteen! Poor, unlucky infant.

WILLUM. *(Coming down* R.*)* Say, what are you people trying to do? Drive me crazy? What kind of a night is this, anyway?

VIOLET. *(Rises)* That voice! *(Sees* WILLUM, *turns slowly to him, cold as ice)* So *you're* here! (WILLUM, *frightened, watches her.)* I understand it all now. You're the instigator of this outrage, are *you?* At last we meet face to face, you blackhearted snake. *(To the* OTHERS*)* Listen, everybody here; listen to me. *(Dramatically pointing to* WILLUM*)* That man standing there knows who ruined my life. He knows the other man dragged me from my house when I was but a slip of a girl in a gingham gown with my school-books under my arm. 'Twas he who turned me into the streets and made me what I am today.

GOVERNOR. What are you saying?

VIOLET. *(Swings around on the* GOVERNOR*)* It's the truth, I tell you. You know that he was responsible for the fact that I stand in the market-place today. But I'm going to make him pay. I'm going to make him suffer. I'm going to drag him down, degrade and destroy him. There's nothing I want but revenge! Revenge! Revenge!

WILLUM. *(Makes a frantic dash for the* C. *door)* Let me out of here! For God's sake let me out of here! *(Unbars door and dashes out into storm.)*

(CRASH.)

VAGABOND. *(Going quickly up and barring door)* Ah, ha! He's gone!

VIOLET. *(Running up to door)* But he shan't

escape. I'll hound him to his grave. *(The Governor goes R.)*

VAGABOND. *(Holds VIOLET as she tries to unbar door)* Take it easy, my lass; he won't get away. *(Leads VIOLET to table L.C. SIX SHOTS. FREEMAN enters on stairs and comes down R.C.)*

MRS. LAMSON. *(Going to GOVERNOR R.)* Robert, this is terrible!

VIRGINIA. *(Crosses and clings to mother)* Mother, Mother! *(At this point WOOD CRASH and POUNDING heard upstairs. SALLY rushes on, screaming, to head of stairs.)*

ALLEN. *(Starts talking off upstairs, then rushes on at head of stairs and comes down R. above armchair)* I won't stand it! I'll not be made a prisoner! I refuse to be held here any longer! What is all this? I demand an explanation!

VIOLET. *(Starts for ALLEN. VAGABOND draws her back)* There he is, the black-hearted wretch; there he is! *(ALLEN intends to dash upstairs, but is halted by VAGABOND'S voice.)*

VAGABOND. *(Holding VIOLET)* Take it easy, my lass.

STEVENS. *(Knocks on door C. ALL turn upstage. The VAGABOND brings VIOLET down below table L.C., then moves to R. of settee L.)*

FREEMAN. *(After a pause)* Who would enter?

STEVENS. *(Off C.)* Open the door in the name of the Law. *(After a slight pause FREEMAN unbars and opens C. door. CRASH. STEVENS enters and stays upstage, looking around without saying a word for a few moments. VIOLET'S face is turned from him. FREEMAN closes and bars door and stays up L. Comes down C., looking at each in turn. Then faces front)* Who are all you people? Where's the landlord? *(Crosses up C.)*

FREEMAN. *(Comes down, slightly back of STEVENS)* At your service.

STEVENS. Who were those two men doing all the shooting out there?

FREEMAN. Officers of the Law.

GOVERNOR. Supposed to be, but in truth they're highwaymen.

STEVENS. Why did they shoot and kill the man who just left the tavern?

FREEMAN. They killed him! William is dead!

STEVENS. Dear as a door nail.

VAGABOND. Dead as a door nail. Lucky devil, died as he lived.

STEVENS. Cruelest murder I ever saw.

GOVERNOR. *(Facing front)* They'll hang for this.

STEVENS. No, they won't. *(Pause)* I shot and killed them both.

ALL. *What?*

STEVENS. *(Pause)* Self-defense—self-defense.

GOVERNOR. *(Pause)* Who are you?

STEVENS. *(Waving* GOVERNOR *aside)* Never mind who I am. *(He turns and looks at* VIOLET, *then at* VAGABOND, *who turns front after a long look at* STEVENS. FREEMAN *goes up to* C. *door.)*

GOVERNOR. *(To* STEVENS*)* Why are you here? What do you want?

STEVENS. *(Silences* GOVERNOR *with a lift of his hand, crosses and touches* VIOLET *on arm. She looks up at him)* Hello, Violet. (ALLEN *comes down to* VIRGINIA.*)*

VIOLET. *(To* STEVENS*)* You dirty dog! You beast! You devil! *(She screams, then faints in* STEVENS' *arms.* STEVENS *lowers her gently into the chair* R. *of the table; wheels, facing* OTHERS. VAGABOND *sidles over, pats* VIOLET'S *hands, is apprehended by* STEVENS; *draws back.* STEVENS *gazes steadily at him.* VAGABOND *goes to settee* L. STEVENS *circles table slowly; sits; pats* VIOLET'S *hands.)*

STEVENS. We've been searching for her since

seven o'clock this morning. She knocked down the guard, grabbed his pistol and made her escape.

ALL. *What!*

STEVENS. Imagines that every man she meets is the cause of her downfall. One of the most interesting cases we've ever had.

MRS. LAMSON. *(Clinging to* GOVERNOR*)* Robert!

VIRGINIA. *(Turns to* ALLEN*)* Tom!

SALLY. *(Clings to* ZACH*)* Zach! (VIOLET *makes a slight movement as though regaining consciousness.)*

STEVENS. *(Patting her hand)* She's starting to come to. When she does I'll put her in the wagon and take her away. *(Slight pause)* It seems that somebody told her Governor Lamson was to pass the Institution on his way to the Capitol. That's what made her so violent. She got the idea she ought to put her case before him. She's the first patient that's escaped from the Institution for a long time.

GOVERNOR. *(Slight pause)* You're lucky to have found her.

STEVENS. I should say we were—very lucky. They do get away sometimes, and they stay away, too. *(Slight pause)* There's one patient been gone from up there over three years. They haven't found him yet. *(Slight pause)* He got away shortly before I went to work there.

GOVERNOR. *(Crosses about three steps)* Gone three years, you say.

STEVENS. Yes. Harmless sort of a fool. The boys up there tell me he was all right except on the subject of the drama.

FREEMAN. The drama?

GOVERNOR. *(Slight pause)* The drama?

(VAGABOND, *after a pause, rises, then goes slowly up*
   R., *gets his hat, cloak and staff and starts for*

door. FREEMAN, *barring the way, shakes head "no."* VAGABOND *turns appealingly to* GOVERNOR, *his hand outstretched, mutely asking for his intercession.)* (*WARN Curtain.)*

GOVERNOR. *(Pause)* All right, landlord; he's a good lad, it seems.

VAGABOND. *(Coming down* C.*)* Thank you for those words, sir. *(Includes them* ALL *in next line)* I thank you all for a few hours of delicious, delightful nonsense. *(Turns to* ALLEN*)* My humble apologies, my aristocratic friend. 'Twas my mistake to cast you for a villain. *(To* VIRGINIA*)* Marry him, Miss Virginia; he deserves it—for he's the quaintest man I ever met. *(Turns to* FREEMAN*)* A word of advice, friend Freeman. Don't tear the young lovers apart from a fond embrace for fear of what might happen to a broken-hearted girl. *(Indicates* VIOLET*)* Behold the sweet maiden of the woodshed. *(To* FREEMAN*)* Promise me that you will not insist that your son shall trade his name for lands and cattle. Your hand. (FREEMAN *takes extended hand.)* Well done, sir. *(Turns to* SALLY *and* ZACH *on stairs)* Sally—Zach—my blessing. *(Turns and bows low to* GOVERNOR*)* Once more to you, sir. Goodbye, and good luck to you always—— *(Bows to* MRS. LAMSON*)* —and to your most helpful wife—— *(Bows to* VIRGINIA*)* —and your extremely charming daughter. *(He comes down* C., *throws his cloak over one shoulder with a grandiloquent sweep, turns, facing the door, his back to audience. Raises staff)* Now, then, Mr. Landlord, if you please. (FREEMAN *throws open* C. *door. There is a TERRIFIC CRASH OF THUNDER as the door is opened. As he goes up* C.*)* Ah, what a night! What a glorious storm! What a blessing to be free on a night like this! *(Dancing around and* *singing)* Goodbye, my lass—goodbye, my lass. *(Continual CRASHES while* VAGABOND *is making exit until well off stage.* FREEMAN *closes and bars door and leans against it as though tired.)*

STEVENS. *(Pause)* Who is he?

FREEMAN. Huh?

STEVENS. That man—who is he?

FREEMAN. *(After a pause)* Oh—just one of my lodgers.

SLOW CURTAIN.

END OF THE PLAY.

"THE TAVERN"

PROPERTY PLOT

Large stone fireplace R.
Large black andirons, grate and gas log (practical).
Large asbestos logs on fire (burning).
Armful of logs off C. to L.
Asbestos log off C., to be put on fire.
Large iron holder for logs R. of fireplace.
Large high-back armchair at fireplace.
One single chair R. of armchair at fireplace.
Table, with jug and pewter mugs, at R.U.
Rough table and 2 single chairs L.
Table upstage L. in front of window.
Table with mugs outside door L.
Pewter mugs hanging from mantel at fireplace and alcove L.
Old-fashioned double-barrelled shotgun below door L.
Old-fashioned fagot broom and bellows at fireplace.
Stairs padded.
Heavy wood bar on door C.
Large wind machine off L. (Used all through the play.)
Small wind machine (loud) for opening of doors.
Thunder drum and beaters offstage R.
Iron plate and cannon balls offstage R. (for thunder crashes).
2 sure-fire revolvers loaded off L.
Tray and four goblets filled with hot tea off L.

PROPERTY PLOT

4 long-handled spoons, one in each goblet off L.
1 small old-fashioned dueling pistol off L.
1 bag of coins off L., also sheriff's badge.
1 large old-fashioned dueling pistol.
1 diamond bracelet; 1 pearl necklace.
1 flask of whiskey; pair handcuffs (practical).
1 rough wooden staff off L.
1 heavy iron weight for "pin dropping" effect off L.
Metronome for "clock ticking" effect off R.; also striking stick.
Clothes pegs R. of door C.; pail of water and sponge off L.
2 old-fashioned rifles for Sheriff's men off L.
Hunting pictures on walls; bear's head over fireplace.
Elk's head over alcove L.; antlers over door up L.
Elk's head over mug up R. seat in alcove.
1 seat in front of window L.; 1 in angle of stairs
Footstool at fireplace; single chair L. of C. door.
Brass tea kettle on chair over firelog.
Candlesticks and candles on fireplace mantel.
Whiskey glass quarter full of cold tea off L.
Wood crash.

"THE TAVERN"

ELECTRICAL PLOT

Baby spot in border to shine off stairs (amber front).
Amber foots and border.
Baby spot in border to shine on table L. (amber frost).
Baby spot in fireplace to shine on armchair R. (amber).
Red baby spot in fireplace for glow.
Rain pipe, hose and tarpaulin off stage C.
Spots R. and L. to shine on rain.
Lightning box off stage L.
Single light offstage at head of stairs.
No light outside door L.
Old-fashioned lantern, hanging from rafters and side walls (electrically lighted; lighted all through play).
Signal box L.1 with 3 switches connecting with 3 lights; red, white and blue, for signal for man on thunder and cannon balls.
Signal light at door for cues for knocks, connected with switch L.1.
Motor off C. with pipes and blower to throw rice at doors and windows for sleet and rain effect; also to blow clothes as people enter from C.

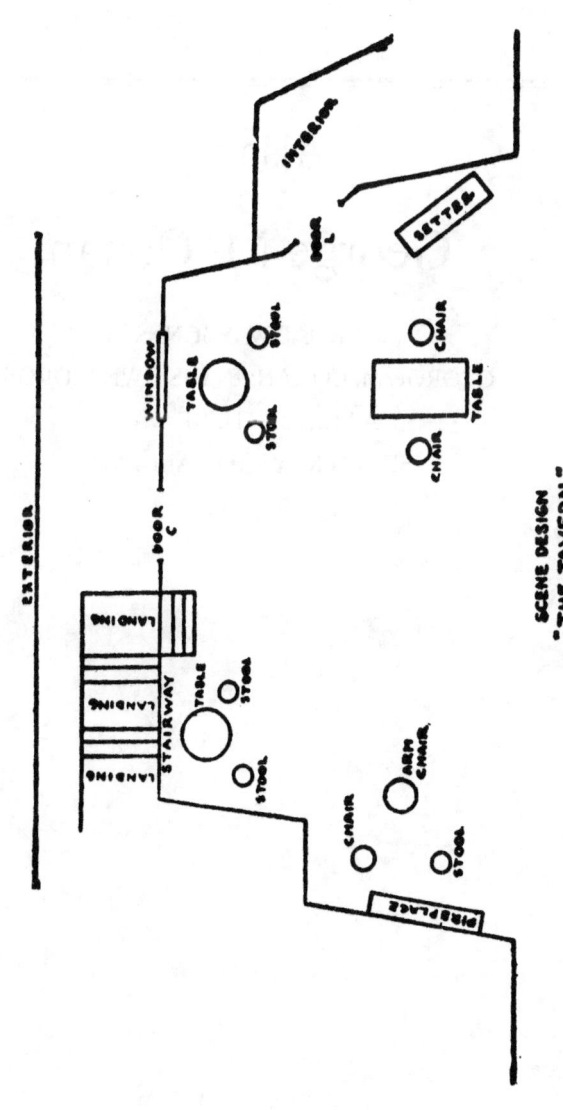

Also By

George M. Cohan

BROADWAY JONES
GEORGE M. COHAN: IN HIS OWN WORDS
A PRINCE THERE WAS
SEVEN KEYS TO BALDPATE

SAMUELFRENCH.COM

OTHER TITLES AVAILABLE FROM SAMUEL FRENCH

DANGER- GIRLS WORKING
James Reach

Mystery Comedy / 11f / Unit Set

At a New York girl's boarding house, there is a newspaper woman who wants to write a novel, a wise cracking shop girl, the serious music student, a faded actress, a girl looking for romance, the kid who wants to crash Broadway and other boarders. The landlady, is the proud custodian of the "McCarthy Collection," a group of perfect uncut diamonds. When it disappears from the safe, the newspaper woman is given two hours to solve the case before the police are called. Suspicion is cleverly shifted from one to the other of the girls and there's a very surprising solution.

SAMUELFRENCH.COM

OTHER TITLES AVAILABLE FROM SAMUEL FRENCH

MURDER AMONG FRIENDS
Bob Barry

Comedy thriller / 4m, 2f / Interior

Take an aging, exceedingly vain actor; his very rich wife; a double dealing, double loving agent, plunk them down in an elegant New York duplex and add dialogue crackling with wit and laughs, and you have the basic elements for an evening of pure, sophisticated entertainment. Angela, the wife and Ted, the agent, are lovers and plan to murder Palmer, the actor, during a contrived robbery on New Year's Eve. But actor and agent are also lovers and have an identical plan to do in the wife. A murder occurs, but not one of the planned ones.

"Clever, amusing, and very surprising."
– *New York Times*

"A slick, sophisticated show that is modern and very funny."
– WABC TV

OTHER TITLES AVAILABLE FROM SAMUEL FRENCH

THREE YEARS FROM "THIRTY"
Mike O'Malley

Comic Drama / 4m, 3f / Unit set

This funny, poignant story of a group of 27-year-olds who have known each other since college sold out during its limited run at New York City's Sanford Meisner Theater. Jessica Titus, a frustrated actress living in Boston, has become distraught over local job opportunities and she is feeling trapped in her long standing relationship with her boyfriend Tom. She suddenly decides to pursue her dreams in New York City. Unbeknownst to her, Tom plans to propose on the evening she has chosen to leave him. The ensuing conflict ripples through their lives and the lives of their roommates and friends, leaving all of them to reconsider their careers, the paths of their souls and the questions, demands and definition of commitment.

SAMUELFRENCH.COM

www.ingramcontent.com/pod-product-compliance
Lightning Source LLC
Chambersburg PA
CBHW070645300426
44111CB00013B/2278